PLANTS & GARDENS

BROOKLYN BOTANIC GARDEN RECORD

ORCHIDS

FOR THE HOME AND GREENHOUSE

Revised and Expanded Edition 1997

Brooklyn Botanic Garden

STAFF FOR THE ORIGINAL EDITION:

CHARLES MARDEN FITCH, GUEST EDITOR

BARBARA B. PESCH, EDITOR

MARGARET E. B. JOYNER, ASSOCIATE EDITOR

STAFF FOR THE REVISED AND EXPANDED EDITION:

JANET MARINELLI, DIRECTOR OF PUBLISHING

BEKKA LINDSTROM, ART DIRECTOR

STEPHEN K-M. TIM, VICE PRESIDENT, SCIENCE, LIBRARY & PUBLICATIONS

JUDITH D. ZUK, PRESIDENT

ELIZABETH SCHOLTZ, DIRECTOR EMERITUS

ALL PHOTOGRAPHS BY CHARLES MARDEN FITCH EXCEPT WHERE NOTED
COVER: *CYMBIDIUM* TIGERTAIL 'TALISMAN COVE'

ISSN 0362-5850 ISBN 0-945352-05-0

ORCHIDS FOR THE HOME AND GREENHOUSE

THIS HANDBOOK IS A REVISED EDITION OF PLANTS & GARDENS, VOL. 41, NO. 2

HANDBOOK #107

Dendrobium orchids photographed in the Longwood Gardens conservatory.

NOTE FROM THE EDITOR

Paphiopedilum Transvaal

Orchids evoke extraordinary imagery—steamy jungles, vapor-shrouded mountain slopes, tropical rain forests. Their exotic shapes, scents, colors, and textures seem unnatural, yet man is incapable of duplicating them. The fantastic array of flower forms, plant conformations, and habitats boggle the mind.

Most of us first glimpsed an orchid on the shoulder of mother or grandmother on some very special occasion. Cattleyas, the corsage orchids, have been hybridized for rounded form and clearer color just for this purpose. For many this may be the only familiar orchid.

The orchid craze began in England in the late ninteenth century. It was the titled and monied who could afford to send expeditions around the world to collect orchid plants and have them shipped back to England—and many plants perished because so little was known about their culture. But some did survive and thrive and were cultivated and hybridized in hothouses. It was not until after World War II that orchid growing hit this country.

Darwin used orchids to illustrate his theory for *On the Origin of Species*, published in 1859; three years later he published *On Various Contrivances by which Orchids are Fertilized by Insects, and on the Good Effects of Intercrossing*.

A great deal of what we know today about the unique mechanisms which make most orchids reproductivity isolated is still attributable to Darwin. There are fascinating relationships between orchid flowers and their pollinators and the adaptations that have been made by both — all of which makes the lure of orchid collecting and growing even more fascinating.

It has been a joy to work with Charles Marden Fitch, Guest Editor of this Handbook. He made time in his busy professional life to gather a world-renowned group of experts as contributors to share their expertise with you within these pages. You will find a wealth of extraordinary orchid photographs, many taken by Mr. Fitch, that are bound to whet your appetite for new purchases. Our special thanks to Mr. Fitch and to all of our contributors.

Whether a beginning orchid grower, or one who wishes to add to accumulated knowledge, we wish you happy reading and good growing.

BARBARA B. PESCH
EDITOR

WHAT IS AN ORCHID?

CARL L. WITHNER

How many times have people asked me if an iris isn't some kind of orchid? No. Orchids are not lilies, amaryllids, gingers, cannas, bananas or irises, but all are closely related. These families are grouped together to form the monocots of the botanical world, and the orchids are noteworthy for having the most specialized flowers, habits and life histories in the entire group.

Flower Characteristics

The major distinction of the orchid flower is the *column*, the single reproductive structure formed by a fusion of stamens and pistils that are separate in the flowers of the other families mentioned above. Though there are basically three stamens and three pistils, usually only the anther of one stamen remains functional, bearing its pollen at the tip of the column. The stigmatic surface, the part of the column that receives the pollen, is just below it.

The orchid flower has three sepals, alternating with three petals. The sepals protect the flower in the bud, but become colored and petal-like when the flower opens, often giving the impression of a six-petaled flower, or five petals plus one that is different. The different petal (and one always is) is called the *lip*. The

CARL L. WITHNER, PH.D., *orchid grower and retired Professor of Biology from Brooklyn College, has traveled, lectured, and judged throughout the orchid world and has written articles for various magazines and books.*

lip petal is marked by unusual form, veining patterns and usually a series of keels and protuberances called a *callus*. The shape of the lip and its callus—sometimes the whole flower—is highly adapted for insect attraction with resulting pollination. In fact, the evolution of the orchid family closely parallels the evolution of pollinating insects.

Fruits and Seeds

If pollination takes place, a seed pod forms that may require as long as 14 months to develop. Usually about nine months will suffice, and the pod may have literally millions of seeds in it. The seeds are almost dustlike in size and are easily carried by wind and water for great distances. The embryo of the orchid seed is so tiny and underdeveloped, in comparison with other types of seed, that special conditions are necessary for its germination and growth (see the article by Joseph Arditti). Until the little ball of undifferentiated cells becomes green, forms a growing point and finally begins to develop tiny leaves, it must live in symbiotic association with a favorable fungus. It is not surprising that from the many seeds produced in a single pod only a few survive to grow to adulthood—a process that may occur in a few months but with most species takes from six to twelve years.

Orchid Evolution

Orchids most likely originated in the warm regions of southeastern Asia and

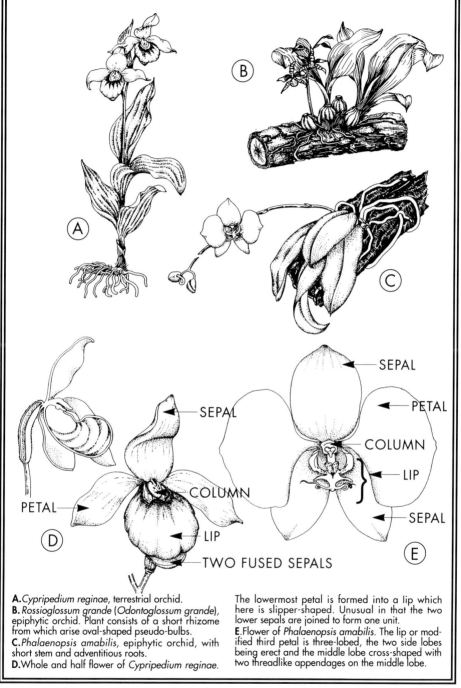

SEPAL

PETAL

COLUMN

LIP

SEPAL

SEPAL

COLUMN

LIP

TWO FUSED SEPALS

PETAL

A._Cypripedium reginae_, terrestrial orchid.
B. _Rossioglossum grande_ (_Odontoglossum grande_), epiphytic orchid. Plant consists of a short rhizome from which arise oval-shaped pseudo-bulbs.
C._Phalaenopsis amabilis_, epiphytic orchid, with short stem and adventitious roots.
D.Whole and half flower of _Cypripedium reginae._

The lowermost petal is formed into a lip which here is slipper-shaped. Unusual in that the two lower sepals are joined to form one unit.
E.Flower of _Phalaenopsis amabilis_. The lip or modified third petal is three-lobed, the two side lobes being erect and the middle lobe cross-shaped with two threadlike appendages on the middle lobe.

ILLUSTRATIONS: STEPHEN K-M. TIM

7

spread from there throughout the world. While the majority remained in the tropics, others, in migrating, became adapted to colder climates by means of seasonal growth that responds to changes in temperature. In the tropics, some orchids can grow more or less continuously, but most are seasonal there, too, responding not to winter *vs.* summer, but to the effects of alternating wet and dry periods. Such factors must be considered in the culture of these plants.

Growth Patterns

The orchid plant itself has a variety of forms that merge into three basic patterns, one terrestrial, the other two epiphytic (*epi* = upon; *phyton* = plant). Terrestrial orchids in both tropical and temperate zones form leaves and flower stalks from underground corms and rhizomes that enable the plant to winter over. In fact, the name orchid is from the Greek *orchis,* meaning testis, in reference to the appearance of these underground parts. Theophrastus, Dioscorides, and other ancients of Europe and Asia Minor were the first to describe such orchids. In those days people were interested in the presumed medicinal uses of plants and whether or not they had souls, and thought that the shape or structure of a plant "told" what it was good for.

In the tropics, the habit of most orchids is to perch on the branches of trees, or sometimes rocks, from which they derive support but nothing else—they are *not* parasites. If the orchid grows constantly from the tip, and propagates itself by forming offshoots (known as "keikis" from their Hawaiian name) from the base of the plant, we refer to the growth pattern as *monopodial* (single-footed). Monopodial orchids are found especially in the forests of southeastern Asia, the Philippines, Madagascar (Malagasy) and Africa. If the plants grow seasonally, responding to wet and dry periods, sending up a new branch each season from the main rhizome, they are considered *sympodial* (with feet). Such orchids are found especially in the New World, but also where the monopodial types grow.

Learning to grow orchids in cultivation and to recognize the different sorts are among the intellectual challenges constantly presented by these plants. No other family involves so many aspects of horticultural activity, from laboratory to greenhouse or garden. No other family can present some 30,000 species and some 75,000 hybrids for the grower to choose from. To anyone who becomes attached to them, orchids soon become much more than botanical curiosities — they are likely to become a way of life. 🌸

Ascocenda Surin 'Talisman Cove'

8

Cymbidium Tigertail 'Talisman Cove'

A HISTORY OF GROWING TROPICAL ORCHIDS

ERNEST HETHERINGTON

There is reason for us to be surprised and, of course, delighted to read an account on orchid growing by a housewife and mother of five young children living right in the heart of New York City. What is surprising is that Mrs. J. Norman Henry wrote

ERNEST HETHERINGTON, *President of Stewart's Orchids in San Gabriel, California, is an accredited American Orchid Society judge, past President of the Orchid Digest and Cymbidium Society of America, and chairman of the Historical Committee of the AOS.*

of her experience in "Garden Magazine" of New York in July 1924—over sixty years ago! She must have been a remarkable woman. Everyone told her that the small six by seven foot greenhouse she built would not work. However, Mrs. Henry read up on the subject of orchid growing and was successful.

I quote, "A little greenhouse does not necessarily absorb much time, a few minutes several times a day and an hour or two several times a year at potting time, is all that it requires. It means also to me that my greatest pleasure is right at my door ready to enjoy at any hour of the day I have a little extra time to spare. That is a great deal, for I have five young children and could ill-afford a luxury that kept me away from them." We further quote Mrs. Henry who said she had been raising orchids for some years prior to her article in 1924, "These first orchids of mine seemed the most beautiful things I had ever seen, and all had the typical fragrance."

It is interesting to note that as far back as five hundred years before the birth of Christ, the Chinese raised certain miniature cymbidiums especially for their fragrance. We shall not go into the history of orchid raising in China. It was really in England and Europe that the marvelous assortment of orchid species such as we know today were first introduced and grown. Vanilla, which is an orchid, was first discovered by Cortez in 1519 during his conquest of Mexico. Plants of vanilla were not cultivated in England, however, until 1739 when some cuttings were sent to England from Mexico by Robert Miller.

The building of the foundation for this modern era extends back well over one hundred years. While there were a number of growers in these early years, they never have come close to the number of growers we have today. Still, it was a different era and the enthusiasm for orchid growing among the wealthy was no less than the beginner with stars in his or her eyes today. Until World War II, England was the homeland of orchid growing in the sense that we know it today. During the devastating years of the war, however, growing orchids commercially in England and Europe was difficult, if not impossible. In Europe, many of the greenhouses were destroyed by bombing. Fuel was difficult to obtain and even if obtainable, the governments

decreed that vegetables should be raised in the greenhouses for the war effort rather than orchids. For this reason, during these years many of the finest orchid collections were sent to America and with them came the interest in orchid growing and the development of America as the center of world orchid growing as we know it today.

We make these comments to gain perspective, for now we must go back to England and Europe and tell a few stories of how orchid growing was developed in these countries. About 1812, some plants of vandas, aerides, and dendrobiums were sent to England from India. At that time, England was the predominant world power and had contacts in all the countries of the world, especially the tropical countries. In 1810, a company known as Conrad Loddiges and Sons began cultivating orchid plants at their nursery in Hackney, England, signaling the beginning of commercial orchid cultivation in that country. Thousands of species were to be introduced and often killed in the greenhouses of England in the years to follow. We say "killed," for as these rare, beautiful, and exotic tropical plants were introduced in their greenhouses, the owners had to learn how to grow them. There was much trial and error.

A Sensational Cattleya

The first blooming of one remarkable new orchid, *Cattleya labiata*, was the most significant event that occurred in the early days of orchid collecting because it developed orchid enthusiasm. This species is a large-flowered purple orchid with a darker purple lip; we all know it today as the purple cattleya. The flowering, we shall call it the "event," occurred in 1818. The plants had been sent to England as packing material by a botanical collector in Brazil. He did not know what they were, neither did those who received the plants in England. William Cattley, of Barnet, England, received some of these strange looking plants with straplike leaves, potted them up and found that they were growing for him. They flowered and the orchid world was never to be the same.

Cattley showed these blooming plants and they were recognized as something new and beautiful in the orchid world. Dr. John Lindley recognized the plants as a new type of orchid and, indeed, a new genus. He described it in the botanical journals and named it Cattleya in Mr. Cattley's honor. Because the purple flower had a large modified petal, which we call a lip, he gave it the name *Cattleya labiata* or the cattleya with the large lip. More plants of this beautiful orchid were sought but they were not discovered in their native habitat for many years. While searching, however, the botanical collectors discovered many other types of cattleyas similar to *C. labiata*. Some of these were *C. mossiae, C. mendelii, C. trianae,* and others. In time, various general nurserymen discovered the beauty of orchids and in particular the flamboyant cattleyas. They decided to establish orchid departments and engage in hybridizing or intercrossing these various exotic and beautiful new orchids that were quickly gaining popularity.

A Duke's Collection

During these early years, orchids were surely not everyman's plant. Through the expanding collection of tropical plants of the Royal Horticultural Society, orchids became more popular and were cultivated by the wealthy. If we search for the spark, the real credit for the enthusiasm for growing orchids in England must be given to the sixth Duke of Devonshire, William Spencer Cavendish. He made the growing of orchids as a hobby fashionable. Cavendish saw a plant of *Psychopsis (Oncidium) papilio* on display at one of the horticultural exhibitions in 1833 and was delighted with the remarkable character and singular charm of this species. The Duke began a collection of orchids at Chatsworth and one of his acquisitions was a white Philippine phalaenopsis which he purchased for 100 guineas, which by today's standards, conceivably could be worth $1,000 or more.

The Duke constantly expanded his collection and sent explorers to the jungles of the world to collect orchids for him. Within ten years, he had the largest private collection of orchids in existence. For many years, as the interest in orchids and the demand for them increased in England, the only plants available were species imported from the jungles of the tropics. As the interest developed also, a number of commercial orchid firms were established in England and Europe which were to become famous. Some of the most exciting stories about orchids were to be told by the early plant explorers who risked their lives going into the mountains and jungles of the tropics both in the New World and the Asiatic countries to bring something new and beautiful to the greenhouses of England. They were professional orchid hunters in the main, employed by the various orchid nurseries. Some had orchids named after them in time such as Parish, Hartweg, Wallis, and Bateman.

The mania for orchid plants in England caused prices of all available new plants to climb rapidly during these years. Auctions were held in Liverpool and London for which $200 was not unusual for a single plant. Some of the rarest specimens, which had been brought in for the auction from the jungles, commanded prices as high as $3,500 to $5,000 at today's values. Famous hobbyists, desiring their names to be perpetuated in botanical nomenclature, bid freely against one another in the hopes of introducing, through their

Phalenopsis violacea, P. fasciata, P. fuscata, P. cornu-cervi and *P. psilantha* are very satisfactory for home growing.

Cattleya Little Bit. Cattleyas have been crossed and hybridized to create many new orchids.

purchase, new species that might be endowed with the new owner's name. It should be added that in the days of the last century, before prohibitive income taxes, there were many wealthy landowners, merchants, and businessmen who could pay almost any price for what they desired and go to any expense to build ranges of glasshouses to house their expanding orchid collections.

One of the most famous orchid growers of all time was H.G. Alexander of

Oncidium Golden Sunset is typical of modern succulent-leaved oncidium hybrids. The plants are generally small and don't require much space.

Westonbirt, England—grower for Sir George Holford. Sir George was a very wealthy man who lived and moved in Court circles. Often he would bring various members of the royal family to see his orchid collection. We read that the orchid displays and the flowers in cut flower displays were changed twice a day in Sir George Holford's mansion. Another collector of note in these early days was Sir Jeremiah Colman of Gatton Park, England. Sir Jeremiah was the Colman of mustard fame. He was quoted as saying, "The money I made was the mustard people left on their plates." "The Orchid World," a magazine devoted to orchids published for some years prior to World War I, carried an interesting story on Sir Jeremiah Colman and his activities. What is of a special interest, however, is a picture of the grand hall of his home which was truly a marble palace of a magnificence such as we can scarcely visualize today.

We ask, "Why have orchids captured the interest of the public almost as soon as the first orchids were brought in from the tropics nearly two hundred years ago?" Perhaps our first answer must be that there is more variety in the orchid family by far than in any other family of plants. The orchids we have come to know are of an endless variety of colors, sizes, shapes, fragrances, and growth habits. Even in the temperate areas of the world, millions of people know orchids from the thousands of species growing wild in the woodlands. We can say they have had their introduction if only to appreciate the lady's-slippers of the northern woods. Even these are remarkable for their distinctive beauty.

The Royal Horticultural Society in England did much to further interest in orchids. At the various shows, private and commercial growers displayed their wares. Even today, the shows cannot be surpassed for number of plants and massiveness of displays. There is an account of a large horticultural exhibition in 1912 in which H.G. Alexander spent months preparing his display.

Propagation—A Serious Challenge

For most of the years orchids were grown, propagation was a serious problem. The tiny dustlike seed was often sown on the surface of the orchid potting mix or on a piece of turkish toweling stretched over wet brick. As the tiny seedlings germinated, they would be picked off and planted. One of the great milestones of orchid history was in 1922 when Dr. Lewis Knudson showed how these tiny orchid seeds could be germinated in flasks of sterile media if nutrients were provided. Here was a means whereby countless thousands of plants could be propagated quickly and easily. The orchid world entered a new era. The orchid world entered another era in 1960 when Dr. George Morel showed how a tiny shoot (a meristem from root or shoot) from a new orchid plant could be taken into the laboratory and propagated in the laboratory.

These little cells would grow and be periodically chopped into smaller pieces. In time, large numbers of plants of this exact variety could be propagated in a short time. The orchid world was introduced to tissue culture or meristem tissue culture as it is properly known. What does it mean? It means that the commercial grower can select a very fine variety, propagate a great quantity of it quickly and cheaply, and sell that plant so that you have exactly what you want at a very low price compared to what you would have had to pay for it before tissue culture.

Where are we in the orchid world today? What is there for you to enjoy? Now you can have, with ease and with relatively little cost, an infinite variety of the finest orchids from throughout the world. Species, of course, are still available in their charming and unusual variations and the modern hybrids are of ever-increasing beauty and variety and many are fragrant. Hybridizers throughout the world are working to create even more beautiful orchids. The beauty is still there; their romance and mystique are still there; all that has changed is that it is easier for you to enjoy.

ORCHID HERITAGE

CHARLES MARDEN FITCH

Orchid growers treasure the original species which come from tropical regions of the Old and New Worlds. In modern times the pressures of development and politics threaten habitats of our most precious orchids, yet knowledgeable individuals in tropical countries often strive to protect the remaining plants.

These photographs feature tropical orchids, wild and cultivated. The survival of orchid species in the tropics is often related to how these species are appreciated by local growers and politicians. Effective protection follows interest, love, and a desire to save the unique orchid heritage of tropical regions. ❦

CHARLES MARDEN FITCH, *Mamaroneck, New York, is a well-known photographer, writer, and lecturer. He is a frequent traveler to the tropics to search for and photograph new plants. He is Guest Editor of this handbook.*

Cattleya mossiae

Above: *Cattleya mossiae,* a popular orchid
often seen in awards judging.

Top left: *Paphiopedilum*
Joanne's Wine 'Krull-Smith'.

Bottom left: *Brassavola nodosa*
growing in its natural habitat in Mexico.

Phalaenopsis growing in its natural rainforest habitat.

THE CLASSIFICATION OF ORCHIDS

PHILLIP CRIBB

Biological classification is the direct result of man's attempts to come to grips with the vast numbers of living organisms in the world. In the Plant Kingdom alone there are estimated to be 250,000 species of flowering plants. Of these, some 17,000 are thought to be orchids according to Willis (1973) and Dressler (1981) while other authorities suggest that this figure might be on the low side. Whatever the exact figure, no one can deny that there are far too many for anyone of us to remember or even begin to know without some help. That help is provided by recourse to one of the many classifications of the orchids—schemes which seek to arrange the various orchids in some sort of easily accessible order.

Simple Classifications of Orchids

Not all classifications are complicated. Indeed some of the most widely used are the simplest and oldest. Every grower of orchid species uses classifications of various sorts in dealing with his collection. He may have several glasshouses each with a distinct environment—cool, intermediate and warm, for example, and will separate or classify his orchids into those categories so that each can be grown under the conditions best suited to it. Even the grower with a single glasshouse will know that some parts of his house suit certain orchids better than others and will place his plants accordingly.

Perhaps the most widely used distinction made by orchid growers is between terrestrial (land grown) and epiphytic (grown off the ground) species. Terrestrials will often be grown in a soil-based compost while epiphytes will be grown on bark or wood blocks or in chopped bark in pots or hanging baskets. All these methods of categorizing plants are forms of classification!

All these classifications are based on one, or at the most, a few features of orchids. Each is useful but only within its limited brief. They are called artificial classifications and often group together quite unrelated or unlike orchids.

The history of orchid classification is one of the production of schemes that tell us more about the orchids incorporated into them. Early schemes of the nineteenth century attempted to group "like with like" while more ambitious classifications of recent years have attempted to group together orchids that are related in an evolutionary sense.

The Species— The Basic Unit of Classification

In all classifications of living organisms, the basic unit used is the species. A

PHILLIP CRIBB, PH.D., *is a research botanist at the Royal Botanical Gardens, Kew, England. He is co-author of* **The Manual of Cultivated Orchid Species***.*

typical definition of a species is that given by Jeffrey (1982) as "a series of similar intergrading and interfertile populations recognizably distinct from other such series, and separated from other such series by genetically controlled barriers preventing interbreeding." For animals, this definition of a species is relatively easy to apply. However, for plants, and orchids in particular, it is often impossible to provide information on breeding behavior and we usually have to rely on the far more subjective notion of morphological similarity to define the species. In other words, if two orchids look alike then they are assumed to belong to the same species, if not, then they are assigned to different species.

This is not always a satisfactory method of delimiting a species because plants of the same species can and frequently do vary, the major causes of variation being the effects of environment, mutation, and genetic recombination. Nevertheless, in most cases, orchid species are delimited on morphological grounds alone. [Classified according to structure, mainly of flower parts. Ed.]

Categories Above the Species Level

The base unit of classification is the species but there are several other categories at higher ranks that are also used. These categories, arranged in ascending order, are genus (plural genera), sub-tribe, tribe, subfamily, and family. The use of a particular category reflects on the similarity and relationship of the constituent elements. Thus species that are closely allied and morphologically similar are placed in the same genus. Some degree of crossability, which in orchids may be considerable, is also indicated. Species that are relatively distinct and not closely related are placed in different genera. The degree of cross compatibility is generally less than between species of the same genus and, indeed, is usually non-existent in unrelated genera.

In orchids, the genera are usually grouped into subtribes, the subtribes into tribes and the tribes into subfamilies. In Dressler's system, mentioned later, there are six subfamilies recognized. Of these the Apostasioideae and Cypripedioideae each comprise a single tribe while the Spiranthoideae has two, the Orchidoideae and Vandoideae four each, and the Epidendroideae six.

The rank of the categories from subtribe upwards can be recognized by their Latin endings as follows:

CATEGORY	LATIN ENDING	EXAMPLE
Genus	Any but usually -us, -a, -um	*Anguloa*
Subtribe	*-inae*	Lycastinae
Tribe	*-eae*	Maxillarieae
Subfamily	*-oideae*	Vandoideae
Family	*-aceae*	Orchidaceae

The Beginnings of Scientific Orchid Classification

The species concept was well established by the time scientists began to realize the wealth of orchids in the world. During the late eighteenth and early nineteenth centuries orchids flowed into Europe and particularly into the British Isles from all over the world. In particular, as the tropics of India, Southeast Asia and the Americas were opened by intrepid explorers and collectors, exotic orchids flooded into Britain and the mania for growing orchids began. John Lindley (1799-1865) was ideally placed in London to see these orchids firsthand and he rapidly became the acknowledged expert on orchids, naming upwards of three thousand species. H.G. Reichenbach (1823-1889), his successor, named many more. Estimates now of the number of orchid species range from fifteen to thirty thousand—far too many for any one person to deal with, let alone remember. The need for classification or scheme to deal with these vast numbers and to bring them down to manageable proportions became ever more apparent. Lindley in his *Genera and Species of Orchidaceous Plants* (1830) produced the first significant scientific classification of the family. The botanical features that characterize the orchids as a family are found in the sexual parts of the flower, in particular, the column that bears both the male (anthers) and female (stigmas) organs. Lindley distinguished seven major groups within the family, based on their column features, in particular the number of anthers, and the manner in which the pollen was held in them. George Bentham (1800-1884) in his and Sir Joseph Hooker's *Genera Plantarum* (1883) expanded upon Lindley's classification to produce a more detailed treatment that was widely accepted.

The first major departure from classifications that relied almost entirely upon the characteristics of the column was that proposed by Ernst Pfitzer (1846-1906) in Engler's *Pflanzenreich* (1895). His scheme incorporated vegetative as well as floral characters. Rudolf Schlechter's classification scheme published in *Notizblatt des Botanischen Gartens Berlin, Dahlem* in 1926,

incorporated many of Pfitzer's ideas as well as those of Lindley and Bentham. Schlechter's classification has been widely followed since it was published. Like its predecessors, it attempts to place like with like by assessing a number of morphological features both floral and vegetative. The result is a useful scheme in which the major divisions within the family are firmly outlined.

The ideas of Charles Darwin on the evolution of living organisms outlined in *On the Origin of Species* (1860) have not unnaturally exercised a great influence over the thinking of botanists. At first, the temptation to suggest that similarity necessarily meant relationship led to various classifications based upon overall similarity being given evolutionary overtones. Convergent or parallel evolution is, however, widespread in the orchids. Quite unrelated species can look alike, e.g., the habit of *Angraecum distichum* and *Dendrobium leonis* and the flowers of *Cattleya, Sobralia* and *Epistephium*. Therefore, more recently, fresh attempts have been made to produce classifications that better reflect evolutionary relationships. Parallelisms, for example, can frequently be identified by assessing large numbers of characters.

Modern Orchid Classification

The most recent and thoroughly worked-out classification is that of Dressler in *Orchids, their Natural History and Classification* (1981). Evidence from floral and vegetative morphology, anatomy, cytology, and crossability have all been used to construct the classification. In it he recognizes six subfamilies. The Apostasioideae, with two or three anthers, are a primitive group comprising two genera seldom seen in cultivation. The Cypripedioideae, the well-known slipper orchids, are similarly rather primitive with two anthers and a characteristic slipper-shaped lip. The remaining four subfamilies, the Spiranthoideae, Orchidoideae, Epidendroideae, and Vandoideae, all have flowers with a single anther. The vast majority of cultivated orchids belong to the last two subfamilies. These contain the majority of the epiphytic species, which themselves comprise the majority of the orchid family. The Epidendroideae contains genera such as *Cattleya, Laelia, Sophronitis, Coelogyne, Vanilla*, and, of course, *Epidendrum* itself. The Vandoideae contains genera such as *Cymbidium, Oncidium, Odontoglossum, Miltonia*, and the monopodial orchids such as *Vanda*, and *Phalaenopsis*.

Although Dressler's system is essentially a natural classification, he does suggest that his arrangement reflects the evolutionary advance of the orchids from the Apostasioideae, with species that have most primitive features, to the highly evolved members of the Epidendroideae and Vandoideae. There are nevertheless species in each subfamily with primitive features suggesting that the evolution of the family has been reticulate rather than straightforward.

New methods of analysis, such as cladistics (a way of constructing or developing ideas about the evolutionary history of a group of plants that can tell us about the evolution of features and hence the classification of the group), will no doubt clarity areas within such classifications as Dressler's. However, it is fascinating to see how much in common his classification has with the early efforts of Lindley.

How a Classification Can Help the Grower

It is easy to see how artificial classifications that divide orchids into such groups as terrestrial and epiphyte; cool-, intermediate- or warm-growing; clus-tered or creeping habit, and others can help the grower. It is perhaps less easy to appreciate how a modern classification such as that of Dressler can be of use to the grower.

The modern classification attempts to place together orchids that are related to each other in terms of overall similarity and in an evolutionary sense. The compatibility of species in such genera as *Cattleya, Laelia, Sophronitis, Schomburgkia* and *Epidendrum* is well known. Not surprisingly we find these genera closely placed in Dressler's classification. The juxtaposition of genera in his classification might well suggest to the hybridizer fresh possibilities for his crossing program. For example, Dressler lists fifty-seven genera as closely allied to *Oncidium* and eighty-six genera to *Phalaenopsis*—surely the building blocks lie here for future hybridizing programs.

Close proximity in a classification may also give the grower clues to the cultural requirements of a species new to his collection or to its sensitivity to various chemical sprays provided he knows the requirements of allied species.

Every grower wants his orchids to be identified and named correctly. It is here that classification and an understanding of relationships can help. If the grower recognizes in an unnamed plant features common to other plants in his collection it will enable him to place the plant in its correct genus or, at least, close by. Reference then to the right section of one of the many excellent identification manuals will usually enable an accurate identification to be made fairly rapidly.

Orchid classification then is a man-made aid to enable us to cope with the vast numbers of species in the orchid family. An understanding of how orchids are classified can help the grower to understand his plants and that undoubtedly will lead him to grow them better. 🌑

OVERCOMING THE PITFALLS OF THE BEGINNER

M.M. BRUBAKER

Considering the ruggedness of the commonly grown orchids and the conditions tolerated in nature — long periods of drought, torrential rains, tropical sun, and almost nothing in the way of nourishment — one wonders why there should be any difficulty in growing them. Some of the difficulty may be psychological. The delicate and intricate appearance of the flowers and the awe that surrounds this family of plants leads the beginner to think that their growth must require meticulous skill. A little study of their peculiarities and attention to a few details are all that are needed to grow some of the showiest orchids. Below are some things worth bothering about.

WATERING • For beginners, the most difficult aspect of orchid growing is watering. To understand this, one must appreciate the difficult transition for the epiphyte orchid from tree limb, where the roots are constantly exposed to air, to pot. The roots must have fresh air even if drying of the surrounding material is necessary to let it in. There is consequently a close relation between potting medium and watering technique. A change in the potting medium usually requires altered watering practice.

Beginners are inclined to make rather impulsive changes in the potting medium. A great variety of media have

M.M. BRUBAKER, *a retired chemist in the research department of E.I. du Pont de Nemours & Company, calls himself the director of a "run-down 50-acre private arboretum" at Chadds Ford, Pennsylvania, where he also engages in orchid culture.*

been successfully used. The British grew magnificent orchids for more than half a century in mostly peat and sphagnum moss. Media as different as lumps of fir bark, fern root, coconut husks, and gravel are used today, and each requires a different watering practice. It is best to stay with a selected potting medium until proper watering has been learned, and then make any change cautiously.

As the potting medium ages and breaks down, watering becomes a much more critical matter. Often the beginner is found struggling with a gift orchid that needs repotting in fresh medium rather than skill in watering. With cattleya-type orchids and many others, light-colored roots "crawling" on top or near the surface of the medium, and plump front bulbs indicate proper watering.

A corollary mistake of beginners, when they realize they are overwatering, is to cut down on the amount of water rather than the frequency of watering. Orchids need to be drenched periodically to leach out any accumulated salts, then allowed to dry out before being watered again.

PROBLEMS IN POTTING • It is a frequent mistake of beginners to change the nature of the potting medium without cleaning out the kind previously used. A particularly objectionable situation arises when a plant grown in osmunda is given a roomier pot in which fir bark is used to surround the old root ball. A fir bark watering practice will then surely rot the roots that are left in osmunda. The old osmunda should all be picked out before repotting in bark. "Potting on," or surrounding the old root ball with fresh potting medium, is an acceptable practice if the old potting material is in good condition, and if the same kind is used. With fir bark, "potting on" is generally undesirable.

FAILURE TO BLOOM • Failure to bloom in healthy-looking orchid plants is most often the result of too little light. There seems to be a misconception that orchids enjoy the gloom beneath dense vegetation. On the contrary, many cattleyas, laelias, dendrobiums, oncidiums, vandas, and epidendrums flower most abundantly when they receive sunlight for at least part of the day. When grown in heavy shade, these plants have dark green leaves and do look better, but the leaves will blacken when exposed to high light, furthering the misconception that orchids resent strong light. It can be somewhat of a task to accustom a shade-grown plant to the high light necessary for abundant bloom.

LET THERE BE REST • It is often essential to rest orchids for good bloom or proper growth. Some commonly grown orchids do not need a real rest, although they have periods of less active growth when they should be watered less frequently. But a bonafide rest period is necessary for such orchids as dendrobiums, catasetums and cycnoches, and some oncidiums and odontoglossums.

Many dendrobiums must have a comparatively long rest period with very dry or cool conditions to initiate flower buds. Often the novice cannot bear to give his plants drastic enough conditions to obtain good flowering.

Cycnoches grow very actively in summer and require heavy watering. They then flower and rest. The bulbs are inclined to rot unless they are carefully dried during the resting period. It is important to wait until the new growth has roots before watering normally.

Many orchids require a rest period of reduced watering to prepare them for renewed activity and to preserve their normal yearly cycle of growth. These come from areas where there is an extended dry season and they usually flower before resting.

STAKING • Tall orchids can become quite disheveled if not properly groomed and supported. Dividing and repotting, particularly, are likely to yield top-heavy plants. For re-establishment, orchids must be held rigidly in the new growing medium. Staking is therefore essential, especially with such tall orchids as dendrobiums and cattleyas. I prefer the type of stake that grips the rim of the pot. It can be quickly made to fit a particular plant, is stable, and can be changed at any time without significant damage to the roots. A good wire bender and some #12 wire will solve most staking and support problems.

FOLIAGE DAMAGE • Wetting the foliage on soft-leaved orchids can lead to alarming disfiguration and serious set-back in growth. The new growth on catasetums, cycnoches, lycastes, anguloas, and calanthes is particularly prone to rot if water is left between the leaves. This is especially difficult to deal with when these soft-leaved orchids are under hanging plants or under a bench. Some help can be provided by dusting the growing cup of leaves with a fungicide. Where possible, however, the best solution is to isolate the plants and keep the new foliage dry.

PRUNING • A fear of cutting up orchids seems common amongst beginners. It leads to unsightly plants, oversized pots, and sometimes advancement of rot. Old bulbs and objectionable growths should be carved off at repotting time. It is best to dry the cut surface of the bulbs or apply a fungicide before potting. Conscientious growers *always* sterilize all cutting tools, usually by flaming, to prevent spread of virus. 🍂

Paphiopedilum sukhakulii

PAPHIOPEDILUMS

THE TROPICAL LADY'S-SLIPPERS

LANCE A. BIRK

Paphiopedilums easily adapt to many growing conditions, including growing them in your own home. They will thrive and flower where many other orchids will not. Even if you have little experience in raising orchids, you will find that paphiopedilums offer some of the best rewards in the plant kingdom. They can be grown in a wide variety of potting soils and under artificial lights. Even some of the rarest species can be grown in the

home, although a few need specific attention at certain stages of their growth. If you have a greenhouse or a separate growing room set aside for plants, your success at growing paphiopedilums will be assured. Another bonus is that there are seldom any insect pests and diseases are rare.

Not only does this genus offer a wide variety of exciting flower shapes and colors, but a diversity of plant sizes and some of the most beautiful foliage in the orchid family. Plants are mostly small (African-violet size) and are attractive even when out of bloom. Plants multiply rapidly and offer the opportunity for frequent division and

LANCE A. BIRK *has made numerous trips to the jungle habitats of paphiopedilum orchids to collect specimens an information for his most recent book,* **The Paphiopedilum Grower's Manual.**

exchange with other orchid growers. With many species a single division can, within two year's time, produce a half-dozen separate growths. During the past fifteen years paphiopedilum species and hybrids have become readily available and can be found in most orchid collections.

Plants can be purchased from orchid nurseries and from mail-order firms as well as from other orchid growers. With all these fine attributes it is no wonder that paphiopedilums have enjoyed a tremendous burst of popularity. There are few plants whose flowers can last for more than a month, bloom every six months or produce consecutively flowering stems. Even with a small collection you can have paphiopedilum orchids in flower every day of the year.

Where Can I Grow Paphiopedilums?

One of the physical characteristics that sets orchid plants apart from other plants is their stomata, or leaf pores, that are fixed open. This means that they are not able to regulate the loss of moisture. If they are grown in an atmosphere which is lacking in sufficient humidity, orchids become desiccated and lose their vitality. If grown in an excessively humid atmosphere they can become susceptible to fungus or bacterial diseases. Generally speaking, lady's-slipper orchids are happy in the same temperature ranges humans are comfortable in, with somewhat more humidity. Ideally, humidity should be at least 50 percent with some fluctuation during the day and night. During the heat of the day humidity drops, but as night approaches it rises and remains high until the air warms again.

Providing extra humidity need not be a problem if there are other plants being grown in the immediate vicinity. Water loss from soil, pots, and foliage furnishes some humidity. In the home, during the drier time of year, or when the heat is on during the winter, grow plants on plastic or metal trays filled with gravel and some water. If conditions permit, you might find a place near a bright window (direct sunlight must be shaded with a thin curtain). Basements can also be utilized for larger collections which can be grown under artificial growing lights. Paphiopedilum orchids are very adaptable for this type of growing.

Nearly all species and hybrid paphiopedilums will grow and flower in what is called an intermediate orchid house. Whether it is in the home or in the greenhouse makes little difference. Ideally an intermediate house will range from 50 to 60 degrees F during the night. A cool house will range between 45 and 50 degrees and a warm house will average 65 degrees. During the daytime, while the sun is shining, a cool house will warm to 70 degrees or more, an intermediate house to 80 degrees or more, and a warm house can go above 90 degrees. It is common for higher temperatures to be found in cool zones, or lower temperatures to be found in hotter areas, and these temperatures are not as important to the plants as are nighttime readings. You can see that the intermediate readings fall within the range of human comfort.

Paphiopedilums require a 20 degrees (average) differential temperature between summer nighttime lows and winter nighttime lows in order to flower. In the home this may not always happen, so special treatment might need to be given to effect this. In the greenhouse it is an infrequent concern because of the naturally occurring fluctuation between summer and winter temperatures. Another problem encountered in growing plants in the home is the lack of sufficient light for certain species, or the lack of total numbers of hours for one or two in particular. When orchids are grown under lights the timer can be adjusted accordingly, but when grown at a window it may be necessary to install supplemental lighting. Usually this is the case with only one or two difficult species.

These orchids need to have free air movement about them at all times. This does not mean that they should be grown in a cool, drafty location, but that they need freely circulating air currents to carry away excess moisture. Leaves should dry off within an hour or so after they have been watered. If you find them still wet hours after being watered, it means they are not getting sufficient air flow around them. At night, when temperatures drop below 60 degrees, or during the day when temperatures rise above 85 degrees, wet leaves are an invitation to diseases. Small fans, placed in strategic locations, will provide good air circulation. In the greenhouse fans should blow directly on the plants, but in the home the lower humidity can cause excessive drying so aim fans to blow above or away from the orchids. In many homes the lower humidity in the rest of the house draws away moisture from the plant room, thereby eliminating any problems of excessive moisture.

Since their light requirements are much lower than most other orchids, most paphiopedilums can be successfully grown and flowered in the home, usually near a window or other source of light. It doesn't have to be strong light in order to initiate flower buds since many buds are initiated by temperature drop and a rest period. Most species are found in rather shady jungle habitats and are particularly suited to growing under artificial lights. Paphiopedilum hybrids have basically the same light requirements as the species. Those species which need strong light in order to flower include: *P. philippinense, lowii, stonei, glanduliferum, randsii,* and *rothschildianum. P. delenatii* is peculiar in its needs. It requires long hours of sunlight as well as fairly bright light, which in northern latitudes may need to be supplemented with artificial means, especially during the winter months.

The best method of determining if your plants are getting enough light is by exam-

ining their leaves. Plants with dark green, droopy leaves aren't getting enough light. They are oftentimes more susceptible to injury or disease and become soft. Leaves which are light green, stand upright, or lie flat without drooping, and which are firm and strong to the touch are typical on plants grown in the correct amount of light. The more light your paphiopedilums receive, the firmer their growth and the more flowers they will produce. As with most orchids, paphiopedilums can be grown in very strong light; however, while they may bloom profusely, the plants will lose their beautiful foliage mottling, become reduced in size and look unattractive. What is needed is a balance between light and shade which will keep your plants looking good and continuing to produce numerous flowers. Paphiopedilum flowers lose their color in bright light, unlike many other flowers whose color is intensified. Also, longer flower spikes will develop in a shadier location so you might find that by reducing the light after the spike begins to develop will bring some much desired effects. Be aware, however, that in too shady a location the flower stems will droop and not stand up straight.

When Do I Water My Orchids?

One of the best means to determine when to water your plants is to knock one out of its pot to examine the root system. Pick a plant at random. Knock another out of its pot, or several others if you are not sure of what you are seeing. Not all plants are in need of water at the same time, but you will be able to notice if the potting soil is very wet, moist, or nearly dry. When you examine the roots of your plant you should look for fresh, whitish, fleshy root tips. There may not be many, but you will want to know if there are none. In this case there might be something wrong with the potting soil, your watering methods or perhaps it might indicate the time of year when there is relatively little root growth. Some plants

Paphiopedilum Tawny Blush
'Orchid Hollow'

normally produce massive root systems while others only make a few roots. This is why it is important to examine several potted plants to learn the habits of each.

If there are decayed roots and a smelly compost, and if most of the air spaces are clogged with decomposed bark or other ingredients, repot the plant as quickly as possible. At this time, it is important to recognize why the breakdown has occurred. The greatest single cause of root loss, and the death of orchids, is overwatering. If this is not so in your case, examine the compost ingredients to see which one is decomposing so rapidly. Perhaps it might be caused by millipedes, which actually eat the compost. Perhaps you have placed a recently repotted plant alongside others which need more frequent irrigation and you unknowingly overwatered it. Maybe you watered the plant when it should have been at rest, or possibly it was placed where it couldn't dry off as fast as other plants nearby. As you can see, you must think like a detective and consider all possibilities. It's not difficult, it just takes a bit of doing.

Paphiopedilums are able to grow well and flower regularly in most any potting soil providing the watering frequency is controlled according to the density of the mix. A dense mix, one that is made up of fine, closely compacted particles, will hold more water for a longer period than a looser mix. There are growers who are "heavy" waterers, those who water often, as opposed to "light" waterers who do so infrequently. A heavy waterer should not use a dense potting mix for fear of smothering the roots of his orchids, and a light waterer should not use a loose mix for fear of starving his plants. If you can be home and in the greenhouse every day you might want to use a loose potting compost so that you can water your collection frequently. These orchids respond favorably to daily irrigation, but only if there is sufficient air movement and if the potting compost allows for rapid drying out.

If your schedule only allows you to be with your collection during the weekends then you probably will want to use a mix that holds water for a much longer period. Remember that these orchids like to be constantly moist, but never wet. Paphiopedilums are able to accommodate a wide variety of growing conditions which makes them ideal for beginners. Let a newly acquired plant adjust to your growing conditions for a few weeks before you change its way of life. If the plant was grown "wet" and you are a "dry" grower, or vice versa, the sudden change can stress it severely.

Well-grown plants which have not been repotted for several seasons will have developed a large root system, therefore need more water. Such plants can easily be watered every day without fear of damage to their roots. In fact, frequent watering may be needed in order to keep the plant growing. Sporadic, or infrequent, irrigation can cause the plant to begin its rest period at the wrong time or the potential for full growth can be limited. You should recognize the needs of these plants and contrast them with another plant which has been recently repotted. A newly-potted plant, even if it is the same size as the previous

Paphiopedilum appletonianum grown by Pat Conley — an AOS award winner.

plant, will not be able to utilize water through its root system until it gets over the shock of transplanting. Time required varies considerably, but you will recognize its recovery when it begins to make new root tips. Newly potted plants will benefit from water being misted upon them rather than having water placed at their roots.

Plants potted in plastic pots will need much less water than a similar plant potted in clay. The difference in water needs can be considerable; as much as 3 or 4 times as much for clay pots. Inside a very bright greenhouse you will find that plants need more water than those growing in more shade. If the temperature remains high during most of the daytime plants will also transpire at a high rate. Air circulation is what causes water to evaporate from the pots and the stronger the air currents, the more water will be lost. Humidity outside the growing area has a great influence upon the rate of water transpiration. Low humidity outside will draw the moisture from the growing area very quickly, and in many instances you will find that trying to maintain proper levels of humidity can be difficult. During the cooler months when the heater is in operation, plants will lose moisture rapidly because of the rise in temperature. During freezing periods the cold will draw water out of the plants and potting soil, then condense on the roof where it may freeze.

Many factors influence the time for watering your orchids. If you pay attention to your plants and "listen" to what your plants are trying to tell you (rather than trying to "talk" to them) you will find that it isn't really too difficult to identify their needs and respond accordingly.

Which Potting Medium Should I Use?

A potting medium must offer support for the plant and keep it in place firmly enough so that its roots will not be injured each time the plant is moved. It must retain sufficient moisture so that the plant will not dry excessively during the interval between waterings. It must also decompose slowly. Ideally a mix should last for two or three years. This will provide enough time for the root system to develop. If the mix decomposes too rapidly your plants will need frequent repotting which will keep them in a state of transplanting shock for too long a period. A potting mix should also be inexpensive enough so you will consider repotting it when it actually needs it, rather than whenever you can afford to do so. Finally, a potting soil should be lightweight.

You will find that there are rarely two people who agree on potting mixes. Each person seems to have his own favorite (for the moment, anyway) and can muster convincing evidence that his plants are doing beautifully in this "magical mix." To all but an experienced grower this certain potting mix might represent the salvation of his deteriorating collection of plants. However, the most important factor is not the potting soil ingredients, but what they do for the plants potted in them. Equally important is the balance between the mix and air movement, light, and the grower's watering schedule, all the other factors previously mentioned. When you find a grower who is doing a great job of growing his plants, do not look at his potting mix, rather look to his methods of growing. Examine his watering techniques and his growing environment. If you find that you would like to copy his potting mix, you must also copy his methods of growing. It may mean that you might compromise somewhere, but that is all right since you must find the combination which will work for you. Whatever you do, you must resist the temptation to try a new potting compound sooner than every two or three years. It takes that long for a plant to really achieve its best potential after it has been repotted.

Among the more popular potting mixes for paphiopedilums is firbark, or other types of tree bark. Medium grade is most frequently used for mature plants and seedling grade bark is used for seedlings. To this bark may be added any number of other ingredients. Perlite or sponge rock, sand, gravel, moss,volcanic rock, marble chips, or bits of plastic chips are among other things commonly used either to cut costs or to add some missing nutrient which the plant might need. One of the most successful and easy-to-make mixes is straight firbark, plasterer's sand and chopped sheet moss. Proportions run approximately 8:2:1, by volume, according to the needs of the species being potted. Plants should be potted firmly using finger pressure only; a potting stick can damage roots. The special qualities of this mix are the variability of the water retention properties, its long life and the fact that it does not seem to produce toxicity as the components decompose. Also, you will find it practically impossible to overwater your plants, especially when you learn to fine tune this mix according to the needs of each species. Best of all, it is a very forgiving mix, particularly for beginners.

Pests and Diseases

While paphiopedilums are rarely bothered by most orchid pests, they are susceptible to some rather troublesome diseases. Fortunately these diseases are not widespread, but only cause problems in certain circumstances. The problem is cultural and therefore not difficult to remedy. When the temperature drops too low and the plants are wet, or when there is excess humidity and too little air movement plants are susceptible to diseases. Both fungal and bacterial diseases can cause considerable damage in a short period of time. Often a plant can be consumed overnight. Some diseases are not so rapid and a plant may be saved by immediate action, but you must act quickly to stop the spread to other plants.

The damage caused by either fungi or bacteria is very similar and, while the chemicals to treat each might differ, the basic form of treatment is the same. Symptoms to look for are brown or black watery spots on the leaf surfaces. Sometimes the tips of the leaves die back, or perhaps the whole center portion of the plant has become affected. These diseases are spread by splashing water or by insects and if any part of the plant comes in contact with any other plant, it too can become infected. The first thing you must do in either case is to isolate the plant. If it has been severely infected and the whole center crown is discolored, it must be disposed of in a sealed container outside the greenhouse, or other growing enclosure.

If only a portion of the leaves has been affected you must remove them with a sharp, clean knife, cutting well into the healthy tissue. If there is any discoloration in the tissue it must be removed and discarded. Paint the cut with a fungicide and move the plant to a shaded location where there is good air movement. Do not water it for several days until you are certain that the disease has stopped. After two weeks you may return it to its growing location, but only if you are certain that there is no problem. An alternative treatment is a drench, where the whole plant is soaked in a bath of fungicide or bactericide, then removed to a shaded location, etc. The drench is actually a more thorough treatment, but be certain to let the plant dry off for six to eight days before watering it again.

Aphids and mealybugs are the two most bothersome pests. A sharp spray of water from a misting nozzle will dislodge most aphids. However, if they recur, or if you have trouble with mealybugs, you will need to use one of the insecticide sprays. Soil millipedes, snails, scale, and any other nuisances can be eradicated with an application of garden pesticide. While these orchids may be exotic, their insect pests can be controlled with pesticides that are readily available.

CATTLEYA CULTURE

NED NASH

Cattleya Susies' Pride 'Talisman Cove'

"E veryone knows how to grow cattleyas." This assumption has probably led to more cultural errors, especially on the part of beginners, than any other orchid myth. It should be stressed that although the various elements of culture will be discussed in separate sections, this is simply for convenience and ease of understanding. All cultural factors are equally vital to the successful growth of the plant. In addition, no one factor may be separated from the others. That is, all facets are interrelated and should be in harmony, one with the others.

Light

Cattleyas require good light to grow and flower properly. Insufficient light is the most common cause of failure to bloom. There are other diagnostic features that will help to clarify the nature of the problem. If the foliage is a dark glossy green and the new growth is thin and weak, requiring staking, the plant has been grown with too little light. The foliage should be a medium olive green and the growths and flower spikes should develop strong and erect, without the need for staking.

Because light is essential to the chemical reactions which produce a plant's energy, a plant receiving too little light will draw stored energy from the older portions to subsist and to "manufacture" new growth. Since there is a net loss in any energy transfer, new growth will become increasingly weak until the plant finally succumbs.

Optimum light conditions will vary from region to region. In areas such as Florida or Hawaii, cattleyas may be given nearly full sun, while in California, plants are best grown with 40-50 percent sun-

Ned Nash, *vice president of Armacost & Royston, orchid growers in Carpinteria, California; trustee of the American Orchid Society; judge for the Cymbidium Society of America and probationary judge for the American Orchid Society.*

light. This is a good example of why close observation of plant growth is a better indicator of proper light conditions than relying on a light meter. In nature, cattleyas grow near the edge of the forest canopy where they receive bright, dappled sunlight. If they are exposed to full sun, they burn, just as they would in cultivation. It is not the light itself that will burn the foliage, but the heat buildup caused by the light. Overheating the foliage is the limiting factor in windowsill culture of cattleyas because it is difficult to provide sufficient light to the plants without overheating the foliage. Even if the leaves don't actually show the symptoms of burning, physiological processes may become so stressed that the plant will grow poorly. This is why the smaller-growing cattleyas are so popular for windowsill culture; it is easier to provide them with sufficient light without overstressing the plant.

A word of caution: plants that have been grown with too little light will burn even more quickly than those that have been grown with proper light. Remember your first day at the beach after a long cold winter? The fact that the dark green foliage will draw heat even more quickly only exacerbates the problem.

A good test for heat buildup is to feel the leaf with the palm of the hand. The leaf should be cool to the touch. If it is warm or hot, the temperature should be lowered. A temporary solution, especially if one lacks artificial cooling, is to increase air circulation and spray the plants lightly overhead.

Temperature

Light and temperature are closely related. In nature, cattleyas may be subjected to temperatures ranging from the low 40's to 100 degrees F or more. Some knowledge of the species background of any given hybrid is helpful in determining which microclimate within your growing area is best suited to that plant. Most growing areas have microclimates that can accommodate differences; for instance, it is warmer near the source of heat, so plants needing more light can be hung near the glass, with plants needing less shaded by the larger plants.

Most cattleyas thrive with a temperature range of 55-60 degrees nights and 75-85 degrees days. The 15-25 degrees differential between day and night is essential for proper growth and flowering. Many orchids, cattleyas included, have a metabolism that manufactures sugars during warm daylight hours, then utilizes them to complete the process during cooler hours. This point is important because unless a plant receives a cool, dark "rest" it will quickly exhaust its food reserves.

It is essential to stress common sense here. While cattleyas require a temperature differential to do their best, do not go overboard. Experienced growers have found that cattleyas do their best if the temperature differential is not too great and the temperatures are at the lower end of the spectrum. The plants will grow best and flower at maximum potential when grown to 80 degrees during the day and 60 degrees (or a little lower) at night. This regime does not stress the plants, allows them to grow under the most favorable conditions, and provides the best flower quality.

Flowers developed under even temperatures have the best size and substance because they have developed slowly and evenly. The commonsense aspect enters when one has to decide the best temperature range for one's own geographic area. Intense fluctuation of temperature is what must be avoided.

It is generally thought best to grow younger plants, especially those right out of flask, a little shadier and warmer. Not only does this give the younger and more fragile seedlings a better chance of sur-vival, it gets them off to a "running start." Grow young plants with 65-68 degrees nights. As they are potted on from flats into individual pots, provide 62-65 degrees at night. When potted for the last time before first-flowering, move them into mature plant conditions. This method pushes the seedlings to an earlier first-blooming, yet gradually "hardens off" the plants so that they do not continue to require the higher temperatures and additional shade.

Effective temperature often consists of no more than proper ventilation and air movement. There should be just enough air movement to eliminate stale pockets of air. This will tend to maintain even temperatures throughout the growing area, and the elimination of the still pockets helps to avoid the fungal problems that can begin in such areas. In mild areas, higher temperatures can be mitigated in greenhouses by having a higher-ridged roof with vents at the ridge. In such cases, bottom vents are a useful addition, as the cool air can rise through the house and out the ridge vent as it warms. This also provides air circulation without the use of fans.

In cooler climates, higher houses are undesirable because of the large volume of air that is necessary to heat. In smaller houses a fan is needed to provide more active air circulation.

With just a little practice, you can readily recognize by "feel" if the growing area is right. The area should feel light and buoyant. The air should be a pleasure to breathe, full of earthy smells with plenty of oxygen. If *you* feel good in your growing area, so will your plants.

Watering and Humidity

The second most common problem is improper watering. Most cattleyas have relatively thick fleshy leaves and thickened stems or pseudobulbs (water-storage organs). Plants possessing such characteristics have them to survive periodic dryness. A dry season in the tropics is one where it doesn't rain every day. Generally these dry seasons are during the cooler winter months.

In nature, cattleya roots are exposed and dry rapidly. The roots will not tolerate extended periods of wetness. The absorptive layer of the roots, the velamen, takes up water like a sponge. When it is fully charged with moisture, no gas exchange can occur. This condition can rapidly lead to rot. Although we generally grow cattleyas in pots for convenience, their need for cyclic drying and wetting remains.

Coarseness of medium for good drainage duplicates the cyclic wet-dry nature of the plants' native habitat and provides the circulation of air around the roots that the plants require. Many growers tend to fuss over the plants and, consequently, many plants have succumbed to overwatering. Remember that cattleyas have evolved to be drought-tolerant and simply will not stand for too much water at their roots.

Several diagnostic tests can be performed to tell when cattleyas need water. Because clay is porous it breathes, hastening the drying of the mix it contains. For this reason clay pots generally require more frequent watering. The "sweating" of moisture from clay pots can give a hint as to whether the plant needs water. By lifting the pot, one can see whether a ring of moisture has been left where the pot was sitting. If there is a ring, there is plenty of moisture left in that pot. A trick that works well in both plastic and clay pots is to insert a freshly-sharpened lead pencil about halfway into the mix. If the wood is dark with moisture when the pencil is withdrawn, the plant does not require water.

Today's lightweight mixes in combination with the lightness of plastic pots can give valuable information on the amount of moisture present in the pot. Immediately after watering, lift the pot; it will be relatively heavy. Lift that same pot before you think it needs water; it should be relatively light. If it isn't the plant doesn't need watering. With a little practice, the weight and balance of a plant in a plastic pot can tell you just how much water is left in the pot.

Very few of us have either the time or the inclination to test each of our plants individually. If the plants are set up with pots of the same size together, and one remembers the intervals between waterings for a given pot size, the initial learning period can be greatly reduced. It is a good idea to double-check your presumptions on watering intervals every so often.

Seasonal influences are important factors in determining watering intervals. Areas like Florida and Hawaii experience seasonal variation in day-length and cloud cover, however slight. As one moves away from the equator, these factors become increasingly important. Plants will generally require less water during winter months owing to the reduced growth rate that results from shorter days, cooler temperatures, and the lower angle of the sun.

Longer and warmer days and the increased growth rate they bring will necessitate more frequent waterings. Many new roots are forming, and increased fresh air evaporates moisture more quickly. It is especially important to take advantage of this quickening growth in cooler or more northern climates. The growing season can be quite short in these areas and it is vital to utilize it efficiently. This requires monitoring the plants' water needs more closely to avoid slowing growth by insufficient water. Only when the plants' water needs are correctly met will the plants perform to true potential.

Adequate humidity goes hand-in-hand

Laeliocattleya Stoned Pony

with proper watering practices. In nature, cattleyas are subject to fluctuating humidity. A good rule of thumb is to increase relative humidity when temperatures rise and to reduce it when temperatures drop. The increase of humidity with rising temperatures will keep the plant's increasing transpiration and water use from outstripping its capacity to supply water from the roots. Lowering humidity with lowering temperatures helps prevent atmospheric moisture saturation which can lead to fungal and bacterial problems.

Young seedlings require more water and humidity because they do not have the well-developed water-storage organs of mature plants. More frequent waterings are required; and if one is fortunate enough to be home to tend the plants during the day, the seedlings may be lightly misted as necessary.

Fertilizing

In nature cattleyas grow on trees and rocks, which provide few nutrients. Fertil-izer comes from many external environmental sources. Birds and other animals leave their droppings, leaves collect around the base of the plants, and nutrient solutions are washed over the plant from above by the frequent rains. Since the nutrients are supplied sparingly by outside sources, we can infer that cattleyas are moderate feeders. Most commercially prepared fertilizers for orchids should be used at one-half strength once a week.

Potting and Mixes

Osmunda, hapuu, firbark, charcoal, and many other materials share the desirable characteristics needed for cattleya potting material. One or another may work better in a particular area or for a particular grower, but all have relative merits and drawbacks. What works best for you and is cost-effective is the best mix. Give a fair trial to any new mix or material. This means a year, preferably two, of using that mix before a final decision is reached.

Laeliocattleya Brilliant Orange x
Sophrolaeliocattleya Jewel Box

It is wise to evaluate a mix *before* deciding to commit any of your plants to it. Factors to consider include: Convenience—is it easy to use? Is it readily available locally and is it likely to remain so? Finally, is it reasonably priced? If these questions can be answered to your satisfaction, give the mix a try.

The majority of cattleyas in North America are grown in firbark and/or tree fern mixes. They provide drainage and aeration, and readily available commercially prepared fertilizers can be used to meet nutrient requirements.

Common sense dictates that a plant in bud should not normally be repotted. Not only will the flowers be poor, but the plant's strength will be sapped by having to open the flowers with little root system. If the plants *must* be potted while in bud, it is best to break off the buds to protect the plant's future productivity. A plant with mature leads that have already rooted is also a poor candidate for repotting. Waiting for fresh root-tip growth or a new growth will help to ensure the

plant's speedy recovery from the shock of repotting.

As one grows and learns from his plants, a sense of what to report will develop. Observation of the plants throughout the year helps the grower to learn at what growth stages a particular plant, or type of hybrid, will sprout roots. Once this is learned, it is best to repot just before the new roots are initiated. This added precaution will prevent the newly emerging and very tender root-tips from being damaged in potting. Many times, if the newly emerging root-tips are lost, the plant will not grow any new roots from that growth and must wait until a new growth is formed.

A plant's flowering season will also influence when it is to be potted. Most spring-flowering varieties root immediately after flowering while fall/winter varieties root when the bulb is barely mature, some months before flowering. This can pose a bit of a problem if the plant begins to root while it is in bud. The only way around this is to pot when the plant is making new growth and hope that the shock will induce it to make new roots sooner than it ordinarily would. When potting, roots should be shortened to approximately 3-4" to reduce the amount of old material in the new mix. With luck these shortened roots will branch, but often they may not. This is another reason why it is so important not to damage the root-tips on the new growth.

One of the most common mistakes in potting cattleyas involves improper placement in the pot. Most people seem to want to place the developing growth level with the surface of the mix at the expense of the back portion being buried. Because most cattleyas tend to climb a bit, that is each new growth develops relatively higher than the last, this habit of potting allows the plant to rapidly grow out of the pot, letting the roots and new growths be exposed to the air and pest problems. More properly, a cattleya should lean across the pot with the rhizome level with the surface of the mix, the new growth nearest the center. The bulbs may lean forward, but the new growth will orient itself upright. It is important that the mix be uniformly firm throughout the pot to prevent any channels from forming where water might too quickly run through.

Pests and Problems

Cattleyas in modern collections suffer from very few pests. Their tough, leathery foliage is not attractive to sucking pests. Sensible use of available insecticides will take care of any minor infestations. It is never a good idea to spray insecticides as a prophylactic measure. One is encouraging resistant strains of pests by this type of usage.

Malathion is the insecticide of choice for most sucking insects. The tough foliage of cattleyas is not as adversely affected by the oil carrier as that of many other orchids, and Malathion is effective against scale, mealybugs, and aphids. (Mealybugs are usually a more serious problem on young seedlings and dwarf hybrids, with their softer foliage.) Powdered wettable Malathion may be indicated in these cases as it does not need the oil carrier. Aphids can be an insidious pest because they usually attack only the flower buds, and these are easily damaged by either the oil base of the insecticide or the force of spraying. Insecticide residues are also undesirable on flowers either. If the buds are not too advanced, thorough spraying with plain water usually will dislodge aphids.

One application of an insecticide will rarely take care of the problem. Most commonly-used insecticides affect only one stage of an insect's life cycle. For this reason, three to four applications at seven to ten day intervals are recommended. We have not found systemic insecticides generally effective for cattleyas (except Cygon for boisduval scale). Our suspicion is that because cattleyas grow relatively slowly, the systemic is poorly or weakly distributed throughout the plant.

Soil-dwelling pests are a minor problem in cattleyas. Snails and slugs do not care for the tough foliage, but they do relish flower spikes and buds. Regular applications of Metaldehyde granules will stop these pests. Sowbugs and/or millipedes occasionally infest the mix. A Diazinon drench will stop this problem. Sowbugs can wreak havoc on mounted plants by eating the fresh root tips. Diazinon or Sevin spray will prevent this.

Perhaps no other subject raises so much controversy as virus in cattleyas. Virus is a serious problem in many cattleya collections around the world, and at this time it cannot reliably be cured. It is very easy to spread a virus from plant to plant, and diagnosis of a virused plant from foliar symptoms is inexact (although you can make a good guess). You *must* disinfect your cutting tools after contact with each plant and heat (passing the tool blade through a flame) is the only sure method. Virus does not necessarily affect the vigor of a plant, although it may. Unfortunately, the more we learn about cattleya virus, the more plants we find infected with it—plants apparently free of the disease. This is probably the most disturbing aspect of the virus problem.

Flowering

It must be admitted here that while a nicely grown cattleya plant is an object of pride to its grower, it is really no more than a means to an end. The plant is grown well so that it will flower. And quite frankly, most cattleya plants are not really attractive when not in flower, even if they are extremely well grown.

Place the plant so that the lead growth faces toward the maximum light. This allows the buds to emerge cleanly and the flowers to open untwisted on the stem. Make sure that the buds do not become trapped in the foliage as they emerge. Many cattleyas will not immediately initiate buds into their sheaths and may seem to rest before doing so. This is especially true in spring-blooming varieties. Temperature fluctuation can cause moisture to build up in the sheath, leading to bud rot. This is often indicated by the sheath beginning to yellow and die. If this happens gently open and remove the sheath, taking care not to damage the young flower buds. The buds will usually still develop, but will need earlier staking because they do not have the support of the sheath.

If the spikes require staking, do it as the stem elongates. Once the stem begins to elongate, do not move or rotate the pot. The plant should be left in the same flowering area until the flowers are fully ripe.

When misting or watering, try to keep water off the buds and blooms so as not to spot or bruise them. Any sort of chemical spray or dust should be avoided for the same reason. Flower buds are very tender and great care must be exercised not to bruise or damage them. What may seem an insignificant nick on a small bud will grow many times larger as the flower matures. Flower stems are also quite brittle as they grow and are easy to snap.

A bad orchid requires just as much time and effort to grow as a good one. With energy at such a premium today, growers simply cannot afford to grow plants that do not perform satisfactorily. Study hybrid lines and growth habits so that your orchid acquisitions can be intelligently, and successfully, planned.

The smaller hybrids available today have many advantages. Beyond the fact that they occupy much less space, their more compact growth habit allows them to receive more light without burning. Many will endure both cooler and warmer conditions than their larger cousins. Another advantage is that the smaller types tend to be more prolific in their production of new growths.

When evaluating a plant's growth habit, whether standard or dwarf, several things need to be considered. A relatively compact and freely branching habit is essential. Bulbs and rhizome should be in proportion to the general size category of the hybrid. A 2" bulb size is no good at all if the rhizome is 2" between bulbs and doesn't branch. Ease of growth is another factor to look for. If a particular type is known to be touchy about when it is potted, it is wise to avoid buying hybrids of this sort unless the other parent has been very carefully selected. Note whether the plant has flowered from most bulbs, or is it a "hit or miss" bloomer? Productivity is an important factor because the best cattleya in the world is no good if it won't flower.

Cattleyas are still the most popular orchids. Their array of colors, forms, and sizes make them a truly versatile group of plants. Outstanding cultivars are more easily obtained than ever, and more exciting new hybrids are being bred and offered than ever before. ❧

ADAPTABLE MINIATURES

H. PHILLIPS JESUP

Orchid horticulture in the twentieth century has been largely concerned with orchids of imposing size in both flower and plant habit. These familiar types, however, were derived from relatively few species in a handful of genera. Despite the public conception of the flamboyant orchid, the fact is that among the approximately 30,000 species of orchids, the majority are small in plant size, flower, or both, and growers who have space limitations or who are simply intrigued with small, collectible things will find a wealth of miniature orchids to choose from. Some have showy flowers so large they nearly obscure the plant that bears them, others have an abundance of small flowers, while some sport an element of whimsy.

A resurgence of interest in orchid species has led some orchid firms to offer a wide selection of the products of evolution, among which are a diversity of small species. As with many other plant families, wild orchid populations are subject to heavy pressure from habitat destruction and over-collecting, and conscientious horticulturists will prefer to obtain their plants from nurseries that have raised seedlings from self-pollination of their stock. The hybridizers too

H. PHILLIPS JESUP, *banker by trade and horticulturist by avocation, has grown orchids as a hobby since 1952. Active in several orchid societies and chairman of the Northeast Region Judging Center of the American Orchid Society.*

have taken note of the popularity of miniature orchids and have been active in breeding for compact plant habit. Their efforts have been most successful in the cattleya alliance, the resulting dwarf cattleyas being known as "mini-catts."

As is true of orchid species in general, the miniature species have evolved under a wide range of ecological conditions,

Oncidium Catherine Wilson
(*O. triquetrum* x *O. pulchellum*)

from high mountains to sea level near-desert; cool cloud forests to lowland jungle; fully exposed lichen-covered rock faces; shaded, mossy tree trunks; tree-top twigs in open savannah forest. Often the plant form gives a valuable clue to habitat, and therefore to culture. Prominent pseudobulbs and thick or pencillike (terete) leaves function as water-storage organs and denote brightly-lit habitat with relatively low rainfall, at least at a certain season of the year. On the other hand, broad, thin leaves and pseudobulbs that are vestigial or lacking indicate a uniformly high level of moisture and shade in the habitat. Culture should dovetail accordingly. Species vary in their adaptability to "captivity," but most are amenable if their particular needs of light, humidity, moisture at the roots, and temperature are observed. Microclimates in the orchid growing area should

be accentuated and utilized. In the home, a sunny window would best suit *Leptotes bicolor* or *Oncidium onustum*, while a Wardian case exposed to good light but no sun, and with the top tipped up for ventilation, might provide optimum conditions for cloud forest denizens and *Aerangis rhodosticta*.

A drop in night temperature of at least 8 to 10 degrees F is important for all orchids (as it is for most plants), and this is perhaps more easily achieved in a greenhouse than in the home.

Are miniature orchids more demanding in their care than their larger cousins? The answer is a qualified yes. While the cultural conditions for orchids from similar habitats are essentially the same regardless of the size of the plant, miniatures require closer attention. Small pots dry out faster than large, and the cork, branch, or tree fern mounts for

Restrepia cuprea

Ascocentrum miniatum

41

some will need frequent watering or misting to keep the plants turgid because the roots, exposed to the air, will quickly dry. A miniature plant with a problem will usually succumb much faster than will a bigger one, since it takes only a few mealybugs or scale insects to suck much of the life juices from a tiny plant compared with hordes for a large orchid. A fungus or bacterial rot can obliterate a little plant quickly if undetected for a short time. Vigilance is important. However, for the enthusiastic grower such extra attention comes under the category of fun rather than work.

Before discussing a handful among the multitude of attractive miniatures, the temperature requirements of each species, which are shown after the botanical name, should be explained.

W = warm (day temperature 75-85 degrees F, night 65 degrees)

I = intermediate (day temperature 70-80 degrees, night 60 degrees)

C = cool (day temperature 65-70 degrees, night 50 degrees)

These are ideal temperatures to strive for, but some variation, as long as other conditions are good, should do no harm. All of the orchids below are, in general, adaptable to home and greenhouse culture within the ranges of their tolerance. They are from 2-8" in height, except for a couple of the oncidiums which are vegetatively small but have bloom spikes up to 20 inches long. Species are listed in order of their temperature requirements, beginning with the warmer growers.

Warm-Temperature Miniatures

Aerangis rhodosticta (W) has a short, horizontal spray of 1-1/2 to 2" narrow leaves with bilobed tips, from among which emerges a bloom spike on the same plane bearing six to ten or more 1-1/4" flat flowers that face upward in a double rank. They are pure white with a prominent orange dot in the center of each. This is a shade-growing twig-orchid from Kenya and the Cameroons, and will grow best with good humidity on a small cork slab or cut section of a rough-barked limb.

Ascocentrum miniatum (W), on the other hand, is a sun-lover. A double row of heavy, stubby leaves marked with dark dots clothe a slowly elongating upright stem. From the leaf axils each spring arise one or two 4-6" "candles" of brilliant, closely-packed 1/2" orange-yellow flowers. The white aerial roots are as thick as a pencil and as rigid. This Far East species should grow well in a bright spot in the greenhouse, on a south-facing windowsill, or close to the lights in an artificial light set-up. A related species is *A. pumilum* (I-C) which is but 1-1/2" high, with needlelike leaves and tiny pink flowers.

Phalaenopsis equestris (W) is a dwarf relative of the larger "moth orchids" which are popular commercial cut-flower and hobbyist plants. It produces a cloud of small rose-pink flowers with darker lips which appear to float on branched bloom stems above the three to five broad, flat leaves at the base of the plant. This one is a bit larger than most of the species discussed, and is of easy culture under conditions of warmth, shade, and moisture suitable for African violets.

Intermediate-Temperature Miniatures

Another relative of a horticulturally important group of orchids is the dwarf *Cattleya luteola* (I). A somewhat creeping species, the paddle-shaped thick leaves and pseudobulbs total about 6" and resemble a scaled-down version of the familiar (and not very esthetic) cattleya growth habit. Clusters of three to eight yellow to greenish-yellow 1-1/2 to 2" flowers erupt from a sheath at the top of the pseudobulb in the spring. The lips are marked with red. This species, found in Peru and Bolivia, prefers a resting period with reduced water after flowering, and requires bright light with some sun to flower well. Pots or mounts suit it equally, but do not over water pots.

Also in the Cattleya Tribe but quite different in appearance are *Leptotes bicolor* (I) and *Leptotes unicolor* (I). Both have pencillike round leaves, the former producing several spidery 2" white flowers with magenta lips, and the latter uniformly pale orchid-lavender flowers about half the size. The leaves of *L. bicolor* are 3-4" in length, while *L. unicolor* is a miniature version of its merely dwarf cousin. *L. unicolor's* rough-textured leaves and its flowers both grow straight downward. For this reason, it should be grown only on a mount, and if the plant is attached incorrectly with leaves pointed skyward, it will remedy that mistake, as subsequently-grown leaves will head sharply down. Both of these Brazilian species need bright conditions and not much water at the roots.

Laelia pumila (I) is yet another cattleya relative from Brazil and it resembles a dwarf version of a standard lavender florist's cattleya. The 4" flower seems enormous coming from a plant about the size of *Cattleya luteola*, and it sometimes outdoes itself by producing two such immense flowers simultaneously from a single growth. Pot or mount culture suits it equally, but the somewhat creeping rhizome lends itself better to a slab of tree fern fiber; it will quickly "walk" over the edge of a pot. Strong light but a less pronounced rest than *Cattleya luteola* will induce flowering.

In the genus *Laelia* are a number of very tiny species which grow in declivities on the exposed rocky summits of several Brazilian mountain ranges. They, along with some larger relatives, are collectively known as "rupicolous (rock dwelling) laelias." Species such as *Laelia bradei* (I), *L. longipes* (I) and *L. lilliputana* (I) have

butter-yellow, white, and lavender flowers respectively, and make entrancing pot plants. Their pseudobulbs resemble green or reddish bullets or marbles, and the extraordinary succulent upright leaves are about 1/2"-1-1/2", although they may grow a bit longer under less harsh conditions in cultivation. Their flower spikes emerge from developing growths and flaunt 1 to 4 flowers which face upward and are of narrow-segmented cattleya form. Bright sunshine and ample water at the roots during the growing season, once the plants are established, are essential.

Neolehmannia porpax (Epidendrum porpax), (I) is definitely whimsical. The species is a mat-forming creeper, each stem bearing a single flower which at 1" is large for the size of the plant. Its dominant feature is the lip which resembles a shiny red-maroon grape, the narrow greenish dorsal sepal and petals framing it like a corona of exclamation points. This Central and South American species is easy-to-grow and prefers to be mounted so that it can ramble. Moderate light suits it well.

From Southern Japan comes *Neofinetia falcata* (I), the "Japanese Wind Orchid," a wonderful species for those who appreciate fragrance. Its cluster of showy pure white flowers exudes a very strong sweet scent at night, sufficient to perfume a room. The lack of color, the evening scent, and the long nectaries lead one to assume that the flowers are pollinated in the plant's native habitat by a species of moth. Vegetatively this orchid resembles a narrow-leaved *Ascocentrum miniatum*, but it does not require quite as much sun. The species has been hybridized with related genera to make a fine series of plants which, although a bit larger, are still dwarf, and bear flowers of rose-pink, orange, coral, and lavender-blue—although with little or no fragrance.

Neofinetia falcata

While *Oncidium onustum* (I) has been known to grow epiphytically upon cacti in dry areas of Ecuador, harsh native growing conditions do not seem to have resulted in a demanding plant. Although it is small, with short, heavy leaves and fat pseudobulbs, both red-mottled, the gracefully arching flower spike can reach 20". It bears many 1" flat golden-yellow flowers in a double rank, the lip comprising 75 percent of the flower. It revels in very strong light, and when it is in active growth *Oncidium onustum* requires frequent watering combined with rapid drainage such as it would receive on cork or tree fern mounts. Water should be reduced after flowering.

The West Indian equitant or fan oncidiums, of which examples are *Oncidium pulchellum* (I), *O. variegatum* (I), *O. guianense*, (I), and *O. triquetrum* (I) are a group of jewellike species. The flower

Laelia pumila 'Dayana'

44

colors of those listed are lavender, white-and-brown, yellow-and-brown, and red-and-beige respectively. Bloom spikes of varying length depending on the species issue from 2-4" fans of narrow, hard, channeled leaves and bear clusters of 3/4-1-1/2" blooms. The spikes often rebloom several times by producing accessory branches. Culturally, they require good light and excellent drainage on a mount or in a very small clay pot, combined with frequent watering. Hundreds of hybrids, many spectacularly colored and patterned, have been made within this group and require identical culture.

Similar in growth habit to the above but very different in flower is *Ornithocephalus bicornis* (I). The tiny, intricate white-and-green flowers are produced from a perfect fan of soft leaves which may orient itself sideways or upside-down. The flower structure resembles a bird's head and beak, and the generic name means "bird head" or, to some, "bird brain"! Shade and moisture suit this species, which is found in Mexico.

Easy to grow and generally available in the trade, *Pleurothallis grobyi* (I) of the American tropics is a representative of the myriad of genera and species in the Pleurothallid group. A true miniature, its wandlike racemes of tiny chartreuse flowers rise well above the 1/4" fleshy, orbicular leaves. Moderate light, frequent watering, and good drainage will maintain this species in good condition on a mount or in a pot.

Trichocentrum pfavii (I) from Costa Rica produces its 1-1/4" brown, white, and rose flowers with frilly lips, several to the growth. The leaves are short and thick, and it too can be grown in moderate light on a mount or in a pot.

Sophronitis coccinea 'Edelweiss'

Aerangis rhodosticta

Intermediate to Cooler

Flowering best in the cooler end of the intermediate temperature range, *Dendrobium bellatulum* (I-C) is a handsome miniature. Stumpy pseudobulbs are clothed with several silvery-gray leaves, and from the top, one or two surprisingly large, showy flowers emerge, generally in the fall or winter. White sepals and petals frame a spectacular lip, which is deep orange at the base becoming pale egg yolk near the end. It performs best with high light and needs a drier rest prior to flowering, corresponding with the end of the monsoon period in its native Thailand.

Dryadella lilliputana (I-C) looks like a tiny green pincushion studded with 1/4" flowers resembling tiny three-legged starfish, yellowish with dark dots. A slightly larger version is *Dryadella edwallii* (I-C). Both occur on scrubby trees in areas of Brazil and enjoy moderate light and a fair amount of water. The generic name refers to the Dryads, the mythical elves of the forest.

Oncidium cheirophorum (I-C) is a lovely dwarf species that is a pleasure to grow. Chunky dark-speckled pseudobulbs and short, thin leaves are the backdrop for late fall flowering of 6" branched spikes holding myriads of highly fragrant small flowers, the mass resembling golden yellow popcorn. Growing on trees along middle-elevation streams in Costa Rica and Panama, this species requires bright light and frequent watering in small pots.

Almost insectlike is *Restrepia antennifera* (I-C). Paddle-shaped, pointed leaves on thin stems support a succession of relatively large flowers from the juncture of stem and leaf, the most showy portion being the lateral sepals, joined in a boat-shaped body with either a yellow or white background heavily spotted with maroon. The dorsal sepal and petals are reduced to threadlike structures equipped with enlarged clublike ends reminiscent of butterfly antennae. Shade, moisture, and moderately cool temperatures will emulate the conditions of the restrepia's native Colombian Andes. This and other restrepia species may be propagated by leaf and stem cuttings, unusual among orchids.

Cool-Temperature Miniatures

For those with cool temperatures for at least most of the year, the Brazilian *Promenaea xanthina* (C) will provide a wealth of proportionately large yellow flowers on a small, neat plant. The plant, too, is distinctive, with gray-green pseudobulbs and leaves, from which the single flowers emerge on short stems. Grow in medium light and with frequent watering for a specimen pot plant with many flowers.

Completing this introduction to miniature orchids are two representatives of the small but spectacular Brazilian genus *Sophronitis*, *S. coccinea* (C) and *S. cernua* (I-C). The former is a 2" plant which becomes smothered with exceptionally showy 2-3" round scarlet-orange blooms held just above the leaves. *Sophronitis coccinea* prefers moderate light and plenty of moisture in small pots, and requires coolness to do well. Less demanding is *Sophronitis cernua*, with clusters of smaller, brick red flowers. It grows at a lower elevation, and does best creeping on a mount. It should be kept rather dry and bright.

The species described above represent but a tiny fraction of the fascinating forms available in small orchids, and the challenge of assembling and successfully growing a diverse collection can be a rewarding (and consuming!) horticultural pastime. ❦

Oncidium sarcodes

AN ORCHID GALLERY

CHARLES MARDEN FITCH

Showy cattleyas, paphiopedilums, and cymbidiums are the best known orchids in temperate-climate collections but many more genera are equally suitable for the home grower. This photo gallery illustrates some of the most charming available types.

Remember that hybrids, even those primary types (between two pure species), are usually more adaptable to variations in culture and environment than species. Most hybrids are thus easier to grow than most pure species. 🌱

Miltassia Charles M. Fitch 'Dark Monarch', top, left. Above, *Dendrobium* Golden Blossom 'Venus'. At left, *Epidendrum cinnabarinum*.

48

Above, right, *Catasetum* Francis Nelson. *Cymbidium* Red Imp 'Red Tower', right.

49

MINIATURE CATTLEYAS

FRANK FORDYCE

What is a miniature cattleya? Presently the major hybridizers of miniature cattleya-types have established their own guidelines of what constitutes a miniature. My guidelines, published by the American Orchid Society Bulletin of March 1983, allocate miniatures to three plant size groups. The micro-miniature, plants of 3-4" in height (measuring from rhizome to average leaf height); the miniature, plants 5-10" tall; and the compact, plants 10-12" tall.

The micro-mini group is currently dominated by such species as the entire *Sophronitis* group, several tiny laelias such as *L. lilliputana, L. bradei, L. lundii, L. pumila*, and others including *Epidendrum conopseum*. Few hybrids to date retain the small stature because, when bred with more full-formed flowers of the *Sophrolaeliocattleya* group, plant size increases. *Sophronitis cernua* hybrids usually do remain small but are very difficult to hybridize. Certainly the micro-minis will find wide acceptance with windowsill and "under lights" growers in apartments.

The true miniature group contains species such as *Laelia sincorana, L. milleri, L. flava, Cattleya walkeriana, C. aclandiae, Broughtonia sanguinea,* and *Epidendrum tampense (Encyclia tampensis).* Hybrids such as *Sophrolaelia* Psyche, *Slc.* Yellow Doll, *Sophrocattleya* Doris, *Slc.* Brillig, *Slc.* Ginny Champion, *Cattleytonia* Keith Roth, and others are being registered monthly.

FRANK FORDYCE *and his wife Madge, pioneers in the hybridization and popularization of the miniature cattleya alliance, are owners of Fordyce Orchids, Dublin, California. A lecturer, hybridizer, and author of numerous articles for orchid publications.*

Compacts encompass the major popular hybrids, with foliage 10-12" tall. The majority of these hybrids have more closely linked bulbs on the rhizome than the large-flowered standard cattleyas and do not outgrow the pot as rapidly. A much higher percentage of award type, full formed, brightly colored hybrids are found in the compact group. Such famous names as *Slc.* Hazel Boyd, *Slc.* Madge Fordyce, *Slc.* Sparkle Fire, *Slc.* Dixie Jewels, and *Slc.* Pixie Pearls are highly sought after by hobbyists. Generally the blooms of these round-petaled hybrids are long-lasting (some up to two months), many bloom twice a year, with a wide range of colors embracing red, orange, yellow, purple, and a few whites. Most can be grown as blooming-size adult plants in pots of 5" diameter. For comparison, the standard, large flower type *Cattleya*, *Brassocattleya*, and *Laeliocattleya* adult plants are grown in 6-8" pots with foliage 14-24" tall.

Scores of new intergeneric hybrids of miniatures are now beginning to appear producing cattleyalike flowers on dwarf-sized plants. These are tailor-made for a grower with little space, such as New York City apartment dwellers; I've seen as many as six hundred orchid plants in in a small apartment.

Miniature cattleyas are among the most exciting new orchid trends today for the hobbyist and home grower alike. If you have ever wished you had something uniquely different to contribute to a conversation, try growing miniature cattleyas; even the most blase will stop and listen. ❧

Orchids under broad-spectrum lights in a New York City apartment.

GROWING ORCHIDS IN A NEW YORK CITY APARTMENT

ARNIE LINSMAN

When I tell people that I grow almost 600 orchids in a New York City apartment, they usually just stare at me in disbelief and ask, "How?" Generally my response is, "Easily." But that's not quite the truth. It is something of a challenge, but there's no doubt anyone—and I mean anyone—can grow orchids almost anywhere; getting them to bloom is an entirely different matter. By and large, those lucky folks who have greenhouses have a somewhat easier time. After all, they have almost completely controlled environments. Perhaps the one major difference in favor of the in-the-home orchidist who grows under lights is that he can provide as much daily "sunshine" as he wishes for his plants.

Starting Up

Before embarking on the highly infectious disease of growing orchids in a New York City apartment, there are certain decisions that must be made. First and foremost the grower must answer the question: Who really lives in the apartment—the person paying the rent or the plants? If you plan to lead a normal life

The late ARNOLD (ARNIE) LINSMAN *grew orchids in his Manhattan apartment for many years. He was president of the Greater New York Orchid Society, a director of the Eastern Orchid Congress and general chairman of the Greater New York Orchid Show.*

in your apartment once you have started growing orchids, forget it. Somehow the plants can take over your life, your space, and your social activities.

Another question is, How am I going to grow—under lights, on windowsills, or a combination of both? There really is no "best" way. If you have great expanses of windows, especially those facing south, and they are not smack up against another building, windowsills may be best for you. But you don't have to despair if you have only north-facing windows. Your orchids can thrive there if you are selective in the choice of plants. However, if you're like me and want to grow all kinds of orchids, you can always supplement the north light by hanging lights above the plants in the window.

Another question—Should I believe everything I read in books about growing orchids? Yes and no. Most books give the apartment grower indications of a plant's natural conditions in the wild. However, most books on orchids, no matter what the title may lead you to believe, are designed for people who grow orchids at home *in a greenhouse.* And unless you are willing to turn your precious apartment rooms into a greenhouse, you really have to learn and devise methods of your own to approximate the specific native habitats of orchids.

Perhaps the most extreme case regarding growing orchids in a New York apartment is that of a man who converted the elegant living room of his posh Park Avenue co-op into what may have been the ultimate space for indoor growing, complete with huge sodium lights, a stainless steel potting sink, humidifiers, air conditioners, fans, and specially lined floors and walls. Of course it cost a fortune, but his plants garnered plenty of American Orchid Society awards because they grew and flowered so beautifully. Sad to say, this fabulous setup no longer exists; the man opted for an honest-to-goodness greenhouse and moved himself and his thousands of plants to California.

Making Adjustments

So the books can give you the basics, but the truth is that you must figure out the best way to grow your plants for your particular conditions, and that takes some time and effort. Among other things, you will suddenly find yourself becoming an amateur plumber, carpenter, and electrician.

When I first started growing orchids, I devoured the books and pored over the photos and drawings, finding most indoor orchid setups somewhat untidy, disorganized, even a bit hazardous. Being reasonably pleased with the look and style of my apartment, I vowed never to have plants all over the place with fans and lights and snaking electrical wires. My apartment, I said to myself, is my home and is going to stay attractive, comfortable, neat, and organized.

Was I mistaken.

It didn't take long for me to develop a serious case of orchid fever, and while the apartment still looks okay (just okay), it has all the ailments I had so assiduously tried to avoid.

There are, of course, ways to avoid a lot of the "appearance pitfalls." One

Manhattan grower has a wall of orchids—shelves of plants with lights above. He can close off the entire growing area by drawing vertical metal shades across the wall. It's very neat and precise, just the way I wanted things to be, but frankly, my hobby just grew like Topsy, and the plants and their needs have taken over. Lest anyone think I'm sorry, I'm not!

Since I grow both on windowsills and under lights, I have different arrangements for the different areas, some of which might strike a novice or non-grower as bizarre. The fact that almost all orchids need light, air movement, controlled variable temperature, water, and humidity in various combinations can lead the home orchid grower to strange solutions. The books—including this one—all have suggestions for achieving reasonable humidity levels; the most widely used is the pebble and water tray. My windowsill pebble trays are, for the most part, dimestore plastic drawer dividers; some have pebbles in them, others not, but all are filled with water and surmounted with rubberized sink racks or plastic egg crating which hold the pots. In some windows I have a single shelf holding the trays, in others there are as many as three shelves. In almost every window (I now have plants in every room, except one bathroom), there are supplemental lights, some incandescent, some fluorescent. All are on timers, set for fourteen to sixteen hours, depending on the time of year.

In addition, there are a pair of three-shelf light cases in what once was a rather pleasant dining room. Shelves and water trays in the cases are mounted at different heights to accommodate varying plant sizes with fluorescent tubes above. And then there are the fans, all over the place, all sizes and shapes, and all operating twenty-four hours a day. In the dining room are two oscillating fans with the two light cases. The dining room window is recessed and has three shelves. A clear plastic roll-up shade can completely enclose the recessed area, providing a contained environment. In the window are two small muffin fans which are "aimed" at the window to "bounce" air movement back at the plants, rather than blow directly at them. Even during the summer months when the window is open, the fans still operate.

Off the dining room is a small bathroom which is tiled, thus providing a somewhat cooler atmosphere. Two shelves in the small bathroom window have fluorescent tubes and a fan. This area has caused more comment by visitors than any other, because for the longest time I chose not to have the constantly-flushing toilet repaired, believing that in its broken state the toilet provided additional humidity to the plants. Now it has been fixed, and I've noticed no change in the plants.

The living room windows provide almost twelve feet of sill space with a wide-open northern exposure. Plants are on water trays, with two large humidifiers below. There also is a brass rod suspended by chains from the high ceiling which provides space for hanging plants and gives a junglelike appearance to an otherwise formal room.

Even the Kitchen

It is in the kitchen that I have had the most fun. The recessed window faces east and has two shelves of plants with an air conditioner below. On top of the refrigerator which is adjacent to the window, is a cool mist humidifier with two fans behind it. One fan is stationary, the other oscillating, gently blowing the mist over the plants, all of which are cool growing. Apparently this system works, since masdevallias bloomed profusely this summer instead of contributing to the usual hot weather funeral services for these types of plants. Of course, I must admit I do not use the oven from April to November, a drawback of sorts, I guess.

There is, in my opinion, no absolute way to grow orchids in the home. Every one I know who grows orchids in the city has a different method or combination of methods to accommodate his or her particular growing locations. Yes, paphiopedilum and phalaenopsis are the easiest of the orchids to grow on windowsills or under lights, yet I know people who grow and bloom vandas with their very high light requirements, odontoglossums with their cool, moist night needs, noble dendrobiums with their light and temperature demands and other orchid genera that greenhouse people say cannot be grown in the home. Yes, it is hard to get a definite, large temperature drop during Manhattan's summer nights without resorting to massive shots of air conditioning (which, of course, dries the air too much), but misting and more fans can help.

Everyone has special tricks for meeting the needs of the plants. They are developed after some trial and error, and since most orchids are both hardy and smart, they tell you if they are happy or unhappy. It's then up to you.

Growing orchids in a city apartment is not difficult; it also is not an easy, passive hobby. You have to work at it. Each of my plants goes to the kitchen sink for watering on a reasonably regular schedule. That takes time, but it also allows me the opportunity to check each plant and its condition, something most greenhouse growers can't do.

Aside from teaching you patience (a virtue in itself in a non-patient city like New York) growing orchids is a relaxing and pleasurable hobby. The challenge is definitely there; the challenge is fun; and the satisfaction of having met the challenge and been rewarded with beautiful and exotic flowers is worth it all. 🍃

GREENHOUSE ORCHID CULTURE

LAWRENCE H. CLOUSER AND MICHAEL S. OWEN

Orchids are a diverse family whose members live in many habitats. In temperate regions, a greenhouse is ideal for protecting countless species and hybrids of tropical and subtropical types that will not tolerate winter conditions. Most of these are epiphytic, meaning that in nature they grow on trees and rocks instead of in soil. Some orchids can be found near sea level and others high in the mountains. There are those that live in rainforests and others in drier regions. As greenhouse growers, we must choose plants that suit our conditions, or create an environment to suit the plants we choose to grow. We must meet basic cultural requirements, such as temperature,

LAWRENCE H. CLOUSER AND MICHAEL S. OWEN, *Longwood Gardens, Kennett Square, Philadelphia. They maintain the orchid collection which contains approximately six thousand plants in six greenhouses, including a display area where up to 450 orchids are used at any one time.*

light, and humidity, and understand how they interact.

Temperature

Temperature is one of the major factors in greenhouse orchid culture. It is generally accepted among growers that tropical orchids will do well in one of three temperature ranges. They are referred to simply as cool, intermediate, and warm. Some growers choose to concentrate on groups of plants from only one temperature range; others prefer some plants from all three ranges. Even in a single greenhouse, we can often find niches or micro-climates that will enable us to grow plants from different ranges. The ideal situation, however, is to have definite temperature zones. It is important to note that regardless of the range, a day-to-night temperature differential must be provided, with the day temperature rising 5 to 10 degrees F above the

A home greenhouse quickly fills with orchids.

night temperature. This is necessary for proper flower bud formation.

In the cool section, the optimum temperature should be 50 to 55 degrees F at night and 60 to 70 degrees F in the day. It is often impossible and quite expensive to maintain these temperatures in the summer, but winter heating bills will be less than that of a warmer section. Many growers use some form of evaporative cooling. The efficiency of these systems is directly proportional to the relative humidity as they do not work as well when the humidity is high. Some growers use compressor-type air conditioning. This is costly and steps must be taken to compensate for humidity loss.

After considering the dilemma of cooling, many people choose to steer clear of the cool section group. Beginners first should try plants from other groups, to avoid discouragement. There are many beautiful and rewarding plants in the cool section (see the table on page 58 with examples of plants and their temperature requirements). Please note that some plants are listed as belonging to more than one section; different species in the same genus may have different requirements. Also, some plants may be on the borderline of two ranges and might tolerate either one.

The intermediate section will support the broadest range of tropical orchids and its requirements are the most easily met. Ideally, the minimum night temperature should be 60 degrees although an occasional dip to 55 degrees would be tolerated. Daytime temperatures should be 65 to 75 degrees. During summer's hottest weather, these temperatures are nearly impossible to sustain. Orchids with intermediate requirements, however, will usually tolerate these extremes. Some growers still prefer to utilize evaporative cooling to lessen plant stress

57

Examples of Plants for Various Greenhouse Temperature Ranges

Cool	Intermediate	Warm
Anguloa	Ascocenda	Angraecum
Cymbidium	Catasetum	Ascocenda
Dendrobium	Cattleya	Doritis
(Nobile types)		
Lycaste	Dendrobium	Phalaenopsis
Odontoglossum	Epidendrum	Vanda
Masdevallia	Oncidium	Vanilla
Miltonia	Paphiopedilum	
Paphiopedilum	Vanda	

during this time.

The warm section, like the cool section, is a luxury to some growers. With temperature requirements of 65 degrees night and 75 to 85 degrees day, heating bills will, of course, be higher. If possible, the warm section should be the closest to the source of heat, shielded the most from the wind, and the best insulated of all the greenhouses.

Humidity

For optimum growth, orchids require a relative humidity of 40 to 70 percent, depending on the temperature of the greenhouse. A general rule of thumb is that the higher the temperature, the higher the humidity. Quite often, we must raise the humidity to these levels, especially on sunny, dry days. The simplest method is to wet down the walks and areas under benches and to syringe the plants. Mechanical humidifiers are available and can be connected to a water supply and a humidistat to achieve a more constant humidity level.

Care should be taken when certain climatic conditions exist. On overcast days, for example, supplemental humidity would not be recommended because there would not be ample time for drying before night, when humidity rises naturally, and diseases can proliferate in overly-damp conditions.

Light

In their natural habitat, orchids may be found growing in a wide variety of light situations. Some epiphytes are found in treetops exposed to very high light intensity, while others grow under dense canopies with very little light passing through. A greenhouse can duplicate these conditions for a wide variety of orchids. Vandas and ascocendas, for instance, have high light intensity requirements and can be hung high in the greenhouse, close to the glass. Paphiopedilums, on the other hand, will grow and flower very well with much less light and can be grown on benches, in shadier situations under the hanging plants. How do we know if a plant is receiving too much or too little light? With intense light the leaves will become bleached and large areas will turn brown and dry. Conversely, if a plant has a very dark green color and does not flower well, it probably is not receiving sufficient light. Ideally, orchid foliage should be light green. Consult reference material for recommendations regarding the specific light requirements for individual plants. Light intensities are generally measured in foot-candles. You can purchase a relatively inexpensive light meter capable of measuring footcandles.

Most orchids will grow well and flower within a range of 1,500 to 4,000 foot-candles. Outdoor light intensities can reach 10,000 footcandles on a sunny summer day and the need for shading becomes obvious, usually from mid-spring through mid-autumn. The most inexpensive shadings are liquid preparations that can be sprayed or painted onto the glass or other glazing material. An advantage with this process is the ability to regulate the amount of shade desired by the amount of material applied. It is usually necessary to manually remove this shading in the fall when natural light is less intense. Another type of shading material is woven plastic mesh which is available in various densities and rated by percentage of actual shade. Finally, there are slat shades made of wood or metal. The best application of this form employs rope and pulleys which enable the grower to raise or lower the shades as outside light conditions change.

Regardless of the shading method used, we must block out 40 to 60 percent of the natural summer sunlight to avoid burning orchids in the greenhouse.

Water

As orchids are very diverse, so are their water requirements. Paphiopedilums and phalaenopsis require much more water than cattleyas, although all three need to be watered regularly throughout the year. On the other hand, catasetums, calanthes, and some dendrobiums require an abundance of water for part of the year and absolutely none for the few months they are dormant. Consult references or growers to find out more about particular plants.

Secondly, consider the environmental factors. As temperature and light intensity rise and humidity falls, the need for water increases; the opposite is also true.

Another factor affecting water requirements is the type of container and growing medium used. Plants in clay pots will need water more often than those in plastic. Small pots dry faster than large pots. Finer-grade mixes retain moisture longer than coarse grades. Plants growing on slabs of cork or tree fern need water more frequently than any of the above, possibly every day.

Regardless of the frequency, watering should be thorough. Be sure to soak aerial roots as well as those in the pot.

Water as early as possible on bright days as this permits plants to dry off before nightfall. Extra care should be given to plants near heating pipes or ducts, or in the draft of a fan. They will dry out extremely fast.

Problems with water quality occasionally arise. Many well waters are very good for orchids and may even contain trace elements. Other well waters may contain toxic compounds such as sodium, zinc, and boron. Watch new root development for an indication of unfit water. Roots will burn and deteriorate when water is unsuitable. Avoid standard household water softeners since they add too much sodium to the water. In any case, seek professional analysis and advice if water purity becomes a problem.

Other Considerations

After meeting the above basic requirements, other fundamentals that may affect success or failure must be mentioned. It is important to realize that orchids do not like stagnant air. Fresh air should be brought into the greenhouse when the weather permits. Even in the winter, many growers will "crack" a vent for a few hours a day to allow some air exchange. Do not allow cold drafts directly on plants. More important than fresh air is providing gentle air movement. This can be achieved with fans. Exhaust fans help in warmer weather as they help remove heat from the greenhouse as well as provide air movement.

Repotting is eventually necessary whether to rid a plant of decomposing mix or simply to reduce it to a reasonable size. The idea of pulling a plant out of its container and cutting it up may be frightening to the novice, but it must be done. Much has been written on potting mixes, containers, and potting methods. If you have never attempted to repot an orchid, read as much as you can on the matter. A visit to another grower for a

Trays of gravel kept moist increase the humidity for orchids.

recommended strength every three or four weeks will suffice. Some growers feel that a high nitrogen fertilizer should be used when plants are potted in a fir bark mix. Slow release fertilizers are also available and can be incorporated into the potting mix or used as a top dressing. A high phosphorus fertilizer may be used to encourage flowering after a plant has completed its growth cycle. This can enhance flower production and quality.

As with any form of gardening, greenhouse orchid growing takes a little time and application. The rewards are directly proportional to the investment. If you are concerned about improvement, read more! Join orchid societies and subscribe to periodicals. Visit the library. Keep good records, as they are a library in themselves. Visit botanical gardens and orchid dealers. With all this help, orchids are not really that hard to grow.

demonstration might be the most informative and reassuring means. Remember that the proper time to repot is, in most cases, after flowering and just before or as new growth develops. Many different potting medium choices exist and even though their properties differ slightly, all are easy to work with. Properties of containers vary, and watering must be adjusted accordingly. The most important factor concerning containers is complete drainage. Slab culture, where plants are attached to and grown on cork or tree fern sections, yields the best drainage but frequency of watering must be increased.

As a rule, orchids do not require a lot of fertilizer. Many epiphytic orchids receive minimal amounts of nutrients in their native habitat. How much and how often to fertilize depends largely on stage of growth. An actively growing plant should be fertilized more often than one that has completed its growth, is in flower, or is dormant. Sometimes overfertilization will cause an orchid to put on additional vegetative growth instead of flowering. When in active growth feeding a balanced soluble fertilizer at one-half

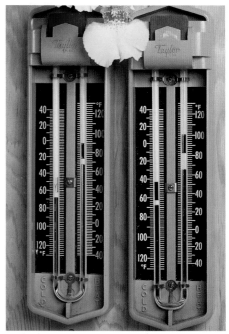
A maximum-minimum thermometer helps chart growing temperatures.

This tree in the dry region of El Salvador supports three orchid species: *Laelia rubescens, Brassavola nodosa* and, in the boy's hand, *Encyclia atropurpurea.*

GROWING ORCHIDS
IN THE TROPICS

CARL L. WITHNER

As orchid lovers soon learn, reproducing natural growing conditions in the home or greenhouse can be a tricky proposition. There seem to be orchid "weeds" that will grow and flower for all without any special care. Others couldn't be more finicky and require a set routine with great attention to detail. A knowledge of such differences and an eye for the intricacies relate to the great variety of environmental niches in nature in which these exciting plants can grow, flower, be pollinated, and produce seed for new generations.

It is amazing how well orchids can grow in cultivation; success with orchids is a testimony to their tolerance and adaptability and of the ingenuity of the growers to provide favorable growing conditions in a variety of climates. A closer look at orchid habitats around the world will give a better perspective on what we are trying to do in the temperate zone, and how we manage to grow so many kinds of orchids side-by-side.

Cultivating orchids in the tropics requires the same attention to detail as in more northern locales. The growth requirements of a given plant remain the same; it's just that they must be provided against a different background of environmental conditions from that of a usual greenhouse, windowsill, or under-light culture. The best green-thumb secret of all is to choose only plants that will grow and flower well in your specific surroundings. Temperature/humidity relationships are of paramount importance, especially in the sea-level locations where many of us live.

Habitats

In the tropics and subtropics most desirable orchids seem to originate in mountainous areas, with relatively high humidity and a 15-20 degrees F drop in night temperature. In the American tropics most cattleyas, certain laelias, many oncidiums, and any number of miscellaneous species come from a moderate altitude, up to 3,000 or 4,000 feet. In Asian tropics we would find many dendrobiums, the green-leafed paphiopedilums, coelogynes, the blue *Vanda coerulea*, and a host of bulbophyllums, calanthes, and still other species. Days are sunny and nights are often cool and damp after the clouds settle down in the evening over the valleys and mountain tops; rainfall may be seasonal. Orchids growing under these conditions are so-called "intermediate" orchids and require a temperature of 60-65 degrees F at night with warmer days. Humidity requirements run from 50-70 percent.

At sea level, on the other hand, especially near the Equator and between the Tropic of Cancer and the Tropic of Capricorn, we find more sun, more heat, and more humidity, with night temperatures about equal to days and little

seasonal change. Orchids growing in these locations still prefer a temperature differential, though it need not be so great. A slight cooling at night will promote flowering in plants such as phalaenopsis (the moth orchids from Southeast Asia), in the cane-type dendrobiums and their innumerable relatives, and in the tesselated-leafed paphiopedilums. Many vandas and their cousins, the arandas, renantheras, and ascocentrums, and all their various intergeneric combinations, prefer equatorial conditions, forming large showy outdoor beds of flowers so spectacular to the tourists in Hawaii, Singapore, or Bangkok. There are no particular American orchids in this "warm" category. Almost all come from Asian areas where they are the most common. The most prodigious of all orchids, the gramatophyllums, are Asian and may reach a height of more than 15 feet in clumps 8-10 feet or more in diameter. Some cane dendrobiums will reach 8-9 feet, and a renanthera I saw was more than 12 feet high. Cattleyas and their relatives do poorly under such conditions, though that is not sufficient reason for people not to try to grow them in the lowland tropics.

At the cool end of the spectrum, the American tropics come to the fore, particularly with odontoglossums, oncidiums, miltonias, masdevallias, the lycastes and their cousins, the anguloas. These plants are found in mountainous areas from Mexico and Central America south through the Andes growing at altitudes up to 8,000 or 9,000 feet and sometimes higher. In Asia cool orchids are best represented by the genus Cymbidium with many species and even more hybrids. There are also numerous dendrobiums, coelogynes, and other rare plants from areas such as the high mountains and cloud forests of Madagascar or Papua New Guinea—areas extremely rich in orchids. I'm always envious of our friends in Guatemala City, in the "Land of Eternal Spring." There the climate, at a mile or more high, is suitable for growing both intermediate and cool orchids, with few accommodations necessary to produce fine plants. The orchids usually reflect these ideal conditions by attaining specimen size and producing innumerable flowers compared with what can be expected in a northern greenhouse — even one with air circulators, evaporative coolers, and all the other expensive paraphernalia designed to provide a "natural" environment.

Tropical Travels

One is always carried away by the apparent ease with which orchids are grown in the tropics, and the temptation to bring them home alive is great. Even considering the possibility of furnishing proper greenhouse or home-growing care, we must fight down the urge to collect! True, people have brought plants home successfully in past years and grown them to perfection, but today it is more sensible to obtain locally grown plants.

Assuming that you have already made arrangements for a vehicle that can traverse tropical roads, have scouted suitable locations with a knowledgeable local collector and have provided for your safety in a variety of ways, you must still obtain that most important document, the CITES (an acronym for Convention on International Trade in Endangered Species) permit, or you will not be allowed to bring the plants into the United States.

Many orchids, as well as other plants, are on the Endangered Species List. Such plants cannot be imported into the U.S. without a CITES permit. More than thirty countries belong to this convention, and even if the country of origin does not belong, the U.S. still requires the permit. Obtaining permits is time consuming, frustrating, and often just about impossible for the ordinary traveler. All of this assumes that you have already obtained your own import permit from the U.S. Department of Agriculture before you ever start on your trip. Locally grown orchid plants look better all the time!

Also, occasionally, it is possible as an alternative to find a tropical nursery that can obtain permits and ship orchids to you by airmail. That is the most satisfactory solution for obtaining a limited number of plants, *if* there is a nursery available and *if* they are able to ship by airmail. But be prepared for the worst, as mail can be delayed in transit, USDA inspection must occur, and plants are not always in good condition on arrival. In any case, they must be re-established in cultivation. It's not with much surprise to say that locally produced plants are often a better buy!

One final word concerns the conservation of orchids. This has become a problem not only for orchids but for all the forests in the tropics—as one author says, "Extinction is forever!" Many tropical ecosystems are currently threatened, orchids included, and anything we can do to prevent these depredations is to our ultimate benefit. We are still discovering and describing new species of orchids and don't know the pollinators of many species; biochemists are just finding compounds in orchids that may be of pharmaceutical value; we still don't appreciate the complete potential of these fabulous plants or many others. Man will have interfered with or stopped evolution in the orchid family in a few short years if more and more forest systems are destroyed. It is more than frustrating to see logged, mined, or other cleared areas with countless orchids just burned up in the slash, unavailable for rescue. Population pressures seem inexorable in so many situations, and our favorite plants are being diminished, little by little, year by year. It gives us an even greater responsibility as orchid growers to keep these plants alive and in cultivation and to learn as much as we can about them in nature so that we can appreciate them in our travels for as long as we can. ❦

A closeup view of *Cymbidium finlaysonianum*, right. Guest editor Charles Marden Fitch, below, in Thailand, holding a *Cymbidium finlaysonianum* orchid that has been cut from a sugar palm.

MODERN PROPAGATION TECHNIQUES

CHARLES MARDEN FITCH

Meristem tissue culture of cymbidiums shown here in a rotator at Stewarts Orchids. Cultures are rotated during the initial stages of propagation.

Your orchid collection probably contains examples of several propagation techniques. Thanks to efficient laboratory procedures rare orchid species, unusual hybrids, and select clones are now sold at reasonable prices. They are propagated by sexual and asexual (vegetative) methods. The most recent advances in techniques involve tissue culture or meristeming, a type of vegetative propagation that produces precise duplicates of the donor clone.

Pure species are efficiently propagated by seed, preferably by crossing two select clones. Superior individual plants can be duplicated with meristem culture. These techniques bring us rare species without threatening wild populations or necessitating hazardous jungle collecting. Outstanding hybrid clones in many genera are propagated by meristem, too, providing unusually fine orchids at moderate prices.

From Seed

For greater variation, with the exciting prospect of flowering something superior at reasonable cost, choose seedlings of new hybrid crossings. Sowing orchid seed is a precise scientific procedure, far improved over old fashioned sprinkling of seed around the base of established potted orchids.

The expert hybridizers and lab technicians know when the fruit (pods) of different genera are most likely to yield viable seed. Picking unripe fruits for green pod sowing allows innovative hybridizers to grow unusual crosses that may not survive if fruits are left to fully mature. Growing orchids from seed is still an important procedure. Through crossing different plants, orchid breeders develop new colors, shapes, vary the season of bloom, work toward improved balance; in short, they manipulate all of the subtle characteristics that go into making a superior orchid.

Vegetative Propagation

Traditional vegetative propagation, the division of plants or waiting for offsets to form, is a slow process resulting in high prices for select divisions. Now modern tissue culture permits commercial growers to propagate thousands of identical plantlets (mericlone plants) from a single individual donor. Growing orchids by tissue culture is similar to seed sowing in that the first few years plants grow on nutrient agar (a seaweed derivative) in glass flasks. 🌱

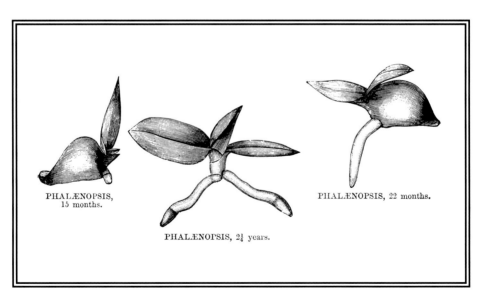

PHALÆNOPSIS, 15 months.

PHALÆNOPSIS, 2¼ years.

PHALÆNOPSIS, 22 months.

Phalaenopsis seedling at various stages of growth.

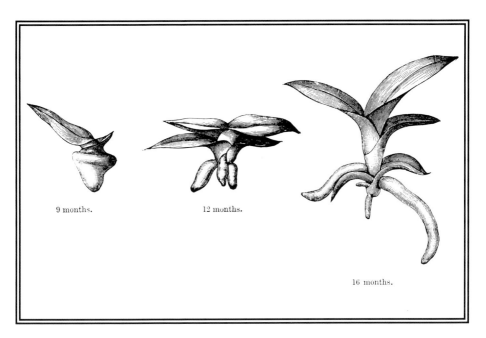

Cattleya seedlings in various stages of growth.

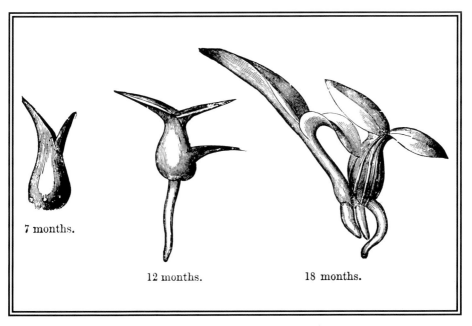

Dendrobium seedlings at various growth stages.

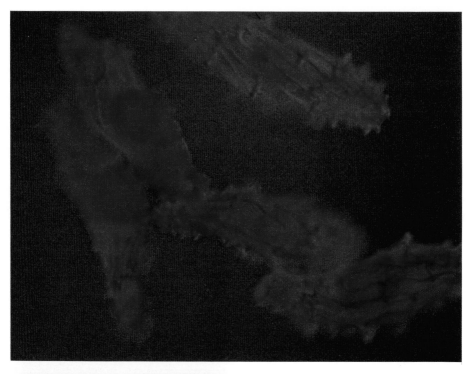

Above, *Catasetum* seed photographed at 400x magnification. Sowing orchid seed is a precise scientific procedure. At left, a ripe seed pod contrasts with a fresh flower of *Brassolaeliocatt-leya* hybrid.

Cattleya hybrid, right, with new growth (1), and two previous pseudobulbs (2 and 3). New roots are growing over the edge of the pot. The *Phalaenopsis* flowers below demonstrate the variation in seedlings produced from the same parents, in this case a pink-flowered plant crossed with a buff-yellow-flowered clone.

RAISING ORCHIDS FROM SEED

Joseph Arditti

The first description of orchid seedlings was published by the Britist botanist R.A. Salisbury in 1804, more than two thousand years after Theophrastus first described what we today consider to be an orchid plant. The variety of false notions that arose in the intervening years regarding the existence, viability and germinability of orchid seeds was undoubtedly due to their exceedingly small size and peculiar germination requirements. Most orchid seeds measure less than a millimeter in length and from less than a tenth to a quarter of a millimeter in width. (There are about 25-1/2 millimeters in an inch.)

The embryo enclosed within a membranous, but often transparent, seed coat is even smaller and may at times consist of no more than ten cells. In addition, orchid seeds have little or no food reserves and appear to be incapable of normal metabolism during the early stages of germination. Therefore, orchid seeds cannot germinate readily in nature. In order to germinate they must become infected with a fungus which somehow assists with their metabolism and may even provide certain nutrients and growth factors. This fungus eventually penetrates the orchid roots where it remains throughout the life of the plant. It is therefore known as *mycorrhiza*, meaning "root-fungus."

Procedures for orchid seed germination were long unknown in Europe, and for many years growers could replace their stock only through importation or vegetative propagation. However, as orchids increased in popularity during the 19th century, attempts were made to develop practical methods for seed germination and seedling culture. The first successful germination of orchid seeds seems to have been by David Moore, Director of the Glasnevin Botanical Gardens in Ireland. He spread the seeds on or near substratum which supported mature orchid plants. A surgeon in Exeter, England named John Haris suggested hybridization and seed germination to John Dominy of the Veitch nursery. He produced the first orchid hybridization in 1852. For half a century Moore's was the only known method of orchid seed germination.

The biological principles which made this type of germination possible remained unknown for many years, since neither the growers nor the scientists of the day were aware of the role played by mycorrhiza in orchid seed germination. This is surprising, because the orchid mycorrhiza was apparently first noted in 1840, positively recognized by 1846, and its existence firmly established by 1886.

The part played by the fungus in germination was, however, not recognized until 1899. The French botanist Noel Bernard and German orchidologist Hans

JOSEPH ARDITTI *is a Professor in the Department of Developmental and Cell Biology at the University of California at Irvine. He is the author of several books on orchids.*

Burgeff, using this fungus, developed the symbiotic method for orchid seed germination. This involved the inoculation of culture tubes with both seeds and fungi. Although this method was a great improvement over the previous technique, germination was erratic and the fungus often killed seedlings. Still, the method was widely used since no better one was available.

The discovery which made large-scale orchid seed germination possible, and in effect revolutionized orchid culture, was made in the United States by Dr. Lewis Knudson at Cornell University. Combining his own knowledge of the influence of carbohydrates on green plants with previous discoveries by Doctors Bernard and Burgeff, Dr. Knudson reasoned that orchid seeds should germinate well on an agar medium containing a balanced mixture of minerals and sugar. He tested his theories by experimentation, proved them to be correct and developed the now famous and widely used *asymbiotic* method for seed germination. Following his original discovery, Dr. Knudson continued to investigate the problem and in 1946 published his improved and by now well known "Knudson C" medium. Although generally satisfactory for most genera and species, this medium proved not entirely suitable for *Paphiopedilum (Cypripedium)* seeds. For these a special medium known as "GD(1)" was developed by Detert and Thomale in Germany. A more recently formulated medium for *Paphiopedilum* by Dr. R. Ernst is more effective.

Seed Germination

The asymbiotic method for orchid seed germination is relatively simple, but it requires care and close attention to details. Basically, it involves sowing the seed under completely aseptic conditions on the prescribed agar medium in a bottle or flask. This is called "flasking."(*) Many orchid hobbyists send their seed to professionals for flasking. When the seedlings become crowded, they are thinned by *transflasking*. When they become so large that they crowd the flask or bottle, it is time to move them to a community pot or flat. This is the point at which most people raising plants from seed acquire their orchid seedlings.

Preparing the Community Pots

A variety of methods and culture media have been employed by various growers. A simple method which was used successfully by Ilsley Orchids of Los Angeles is to fill a 5-inch pot with coarse fir bark or broken clay pots to within 1-1/2-2 inches from the top. This insures good drainage. Each pot is then filled to its rim with a well mixed, thoroughly moistened, firmly tamped compost consisting of the following:

seedling grade, heat-treated, kiln dried fir bark	80-90% by volume
shredded redwood bark or redwood shavings	10-20% by volume
Dolomitic limestone	a full 4-inch pot per 2 cu. ft.
hoof and horn meal	the same

Removal and Preparation of Seedlings

Soften the agar by placing the bottles in body-temperature water for 30-60 minutes. The seedlings can then be easily pulled out with a wire loop. If they are

Paphiopedilum rothschildianum
germinating seeds.

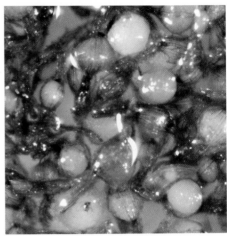

Paphiopedilum rothschildianum
protocorms.

too big, break the bottles. Soak or wash the seedlings in lukewarm water until *all* the agar has been removed. This should be followed by a rinse in a good anti-damp agent (a fungicide) according to the instructions on the package.

Planting the Seedlings

Make a deep hole with a stick about the diameter of a pencil, carefully insert the seedling in it and firm the compost around all the roots. Allow about 1-1/2-2 square inches per seedling, and there probably will be no need to repeat until they reach 6 inches in height.

Growing the Seedlings

Place the community pots in a corner of the greenhouse where the light intensity is about 1,000 foot candles. Day temperatures should be about 75 degrees F but no higher than 90 degrees F, and the night minimum not below 70 degrees F. Relative humidity should be around 70 percent. The young seedlings should be sprayed with a fine mist two or three times a day. Do not water them

during the first week. After that, water *carefully*, since over-watering is the most common cause of failure. When young roots appear on the seedlings (usually within two to four weeks), it is time to start fertilizing. Use any of the commercial high-nitrogen soluble fertilizers, either at quarter strength once a week or 1/10 or less strength with every watering. Leach the compost every two to three weeks to prevent build-up of salts. When the seedlings become crowded, it is time to move them to separate pots. Fir bark, Mexican tree fern or Hawaiian hapuu may be used for this purpose. Pack the potting material lightly around the roots, taking care not to damage the roots. Place the pots on a greenhouse bench and treat them as adult plants. Good luck!

Research support by the American Orchid Society and the Orchid Digest Corporation have made the writing of this possible. I would also like to thank Lynn Maxey and Robert Knauft for their aid in the preparation of the article.

The dorsal sepals of this *Cattleya* hybrid show evidence of air pollution.

CONTROL OF COMMON ORCHID PESTS

CHARLES MARDEN FITCH

The usual array of houseplant pests infest orchids. Flower buds are favored by aphids, new growth and roots may be attacked by mealybugs, and scale insects occasionally establish on pseudobulbs. New root tips and tender sprouting inflorescences are eaten by slugs and snails. Spider-mites often gather on thin-leaved orchids but some mites damage even the thicker-leaved phalaenopsis. Beetles and weevils may invade a collection to feast on new leaves or flowers. All of these

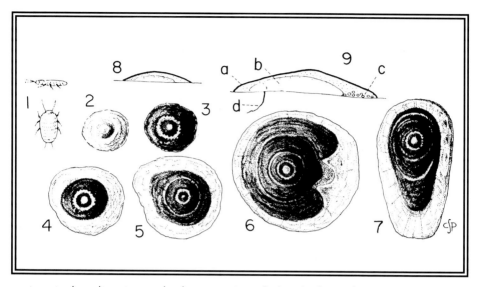

Armored or diaspine scale showing 1) newly hatched crawler, 2 to 5) growth stages, 6) mature female, 7) male, 8) longitudinal section of young scale and 9) longitudinal section of mature female showing a) scale covering, b) actual body of scale, c) eggs in space between body and cover and d) mouthparts which penetrate plant.

pests can become serious threats to orchid plant health unless you control them.

General Recommendations

1. Follow pesticide directions. Never mix sprays at concentrations stronger than suggested.

2. Wettable or soluble powders are preferable to emulsified liquid pesticides. The liquid preparations often contain an oil base carrier that may harm some orchids.

3. Apply pesticides thoroughly, but not enough to saturate the root area unless you are using a product specified as a drench for root-dwelling pests.

4. Re-apply the appropriate pesticide a second time in seven to ten days, or as recommended on the package. Most preparations kill adult pests but not the eggs.

5. Inspect newly acquired plants for pests. Isolate new plants for a month, then inspect again for pests. Placing newly acquired plants directly next to other specimens in your collection is a good way to introduce pests.

Pest Controls

Aphids: Wash off exposed insects. Spray orchids with Malathion or Orthene soluble powder (1 teaspoon per gallon of water).

Caterpillars: The biological insecticide made with *Bacillus thuringiensis* is very safe. It is available as Thuricide, Reuter Caterpillar Attack, and other brands. Soluble Orthene powder mixed one teaspoon per gallon of water is also useful.

Mealybugs: Add a few drops of wetting agent per gallon of spray to help insecticide get through waxy covering of these pests. Malathion and Orthene soluble powder are effective.

Mites: Pentac powder and Kelthane are useful miticides. Be sure to get spray on undersides of foliage.

Scale: Diazinon, Malathion, or Orthene soluble powder will kill crawling stages of scale. Add wetting agent and repeat application according to package instructions.

Snails and Slugs: Use safe solid bait pellets around pots. Spray potting mix with metaldehyde snail/slug pesticide or sprinkle granular form on surface of potting mix.

Orchid Diseases

The best way to avoid orchid diseases is to be sure all plants added to your collection are disease-free. Keep your orchids healthy by controlling pests and growing the plants with adequate air circulation and light. Water early in the day so that foliage is dry by nightfall. The lower temperatures at night, coupled with darkness, encourage diseases to start if foliage is wet or water rests in new growth.

Even with careful cultivation some disease is bound to occur on a few plants. In fact some orchids are more susceptible to bacterial and fungus disease than others. With two different cattleya hybrids grown side by side one may get rot (a *Pythium* or *Phytophthora* fungus attack) while the other remains healthy. If you find that certain clones are prone to disease under the conditions you can provide, consider growing plants that are better adapted to your environment.

Fungus diseases such as black rot (*Phytophthora cactorum* and *Phythium ultimum*) and anthracnose (*Glomerella* sp.) are easy for non-specialists to confuse with bacterial diseases such as brown spot (*Pseudomonas* sp. and *Erwinia* sp.). Both fungus and bacterial diseases may occur in a collection. Fortunately some modern sprays such as Banrot, Natriphrene, and Physan help control both types of diseases.

Physan liquid, mixed 1 to 1-1/2 teaspoons per gallon of water is effective in preventing some troublesome bacterial rots that attack seedlings, especially *Phalaenopsis*. Plant pathologist and orchid disease expert, Harry C. Burnett of the Florida Department of Agriculture, recommends a spray of benomyl 50 percent wettable powder (sold as Benlate) at 1 tablespoon per gallon of water to control several common diseases such as anthracnose, leafspot, fusarium wilt, and botrytis petal blight. He also confirms that Physan is useful in preventing damp-off of seedlings just transplanted from flasks, and community-pot sized seedlings when used as a drench every two weeks (1-1/2 teaspoons of Physan per gallon of water). For many illustrations of orchid diseases see the booklet *Orchid Diseases* by Harry C. Burnett, published as Bulletin No. 10 of the Florida Department of Agriculture, a publication available in most botanical garden libraries. 🌱

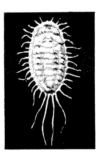

Mealybug

75

The flower of this *Cattleya* hybrid has been damaged by slugs.

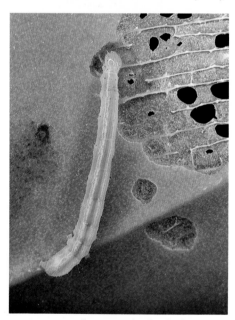

Caterpillar eats the leaf of a *Phalaenopsis* orchid.

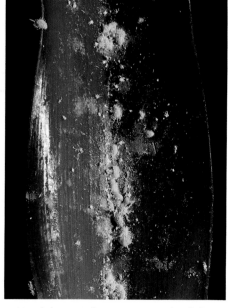

Mealybugs infest new growth of this *Cattleya* hybrid.

BENEFITS OF THE AOS AWARDS SYSTEM

ERNEST HETHERINGTON

The American Orchid Society national system of awards began in the first years after World War II. Since 1945 the AOS has developed an internationally recognized system to meet the need for a fair method of evaluating orchids. The AOS Awards system is fully detailed in the AOS "Handbook on Judg-

ing." How does this awards system benefit the amateur grower?

The Judging System

Even a beginner when selecting an orchid asks, "How does this orchid, which I now have in bloom, compare in quality and other desirable characteris-

American Orchid Society judges study a *Pleurothallis* species at its monthly session.

tics with others of its type?" We could put the question another way: "How do I tell a good orchid from a bad one?" The AOS awards system helps answer these questions.

The AOS system of judging grants awards in several categories. The first category grants recognition to a superior form of an existent type. To illustrate: if you have a purple *Cattleya*, what are the qualities for perfection in that type to look for? Our second judging area is to grant recognition to new orchid hybrids that are not only new but desirably different, or an improvement. Hybridizers are continually inter-crossing a great variety of dissimilar orchids. When a distinctly different orchid comes along, one that also has charm and beauty, it is worthy of recognition. Our third category is to grant recognition to superior forms of species which have been collected from jungles around the world. If we study orchids in nature, we find that even within a given species, not all are alike. Sometimes one particular plant in a group will have flowers that are larger or darker or have certain characteristics that stand out. The Society grants recognition to these plants if shown before an AOS judging panel.

We must mention, in discussing our judging system, that there are two types of judging. Many amateurs are familiar with ribbon awards given at flower shows. These are for the first, second, or third prize at that show. The awards apply only to plants submitted at that show. The AOS system, however, is based upon evaluating that plant in bloom against all others of that basic type which the judges *may have seen*; this requires experience. It is the only fair method of granting recognition. The AOS system was patterned after judging of the Royal Horticultural Society in England which has been granting awards since 1859. Most of the orchids which are grown today are

hybrids. They are the work of orchid breeders who create not only new types of orchids but who also improve existing types. The quality of our orchids is constantly improving. Even as they improve, there is no final perfection.

There are over four hundred AOS judges throughout America. A minimum of six years of training; three years as a student judge and three years as a probationary judge, are required before a person is given the title "Accredited AOS Judge." There are eighteen regional judging centers throughout the United States. The American Orchid Society Bulletin lists the location of these judging centers. These comments are intended to place emphasis on how an awards system can be of benefit to you. If there is a judging center near you, attend a session to see how orchids are judged. If you have a plant you think might be worthy of an award, take it in. There is no charge for having it judged. If it gets an award, there is a small clerical charge. When you submit the plant, you will be required to fill out an entry form. The plant is then screened by a panel of judges. If they think it should be judged, it is scored by not fewer than three judges. When we say screened, they collectively look at it. If they think it stands a chance of receiving 75 points, this is the minimum number of points required for an award, they send it to a judging panel.

What is important to you as an amateur is that when a plant receives an award from the American Orchid Society, it keeps that award forever. If it is divided into any number of divisions, every division carries the same name and the award that your plant received. This is why awards are of value to an amateur grower. If you are offered a plant or have the opportunity to buy one at a commercial nursery which has received an award, you know that it has been judged by an impartial panel and the quality of the flower meets certain American Orchid Society standards.

Some Criteria for Judging

In discussing the practical value of an award system, surely the question must be asked, "What do I look for in various orchids to determine their quality?" The major genera grown in the United States are cattleyas and allied hybrids, paphiopedilums (lady slippers), phalaenopsis, cymbidiums, oncidiums, odontoglossums, vandas, and dendrobiums.

In cattleyas, look for good flower qualities. The color must be intense, clear, and rich. The shape should be round and full with flatness and symmetry. If it is a large-flowered type, the flowers should be of good size. What is important, also, is that the flower should be carried well on a good, strong stem. Those cattleyas with small flowers must have the qualities described above except for size of flower.

Phalaenopsis have flowers of white and pink, which can now be expected to have large size and good rich coloring with flowers well carried on a strong stem. White phalaenopsis should have good coloration and substance so that they are not transparent. Striped or spotted phalaenopsis should have rich colors with clear, sharp markings.

In paphiopedilums look for large size, good carriage, and richness of color. The flowers (generally they have one flower to the stem) should be carried erectly on a good, strong stem. There are several basic types—the sort with spotting on the flower parts. The spotting should be clear, distinct, and bold. If it is a flower without spotting, intensity and clearness of coloring are the qualities that separate the average from the superior flower.

Millions of cymbidiums are grown throughout America, in both conventional and miniature types. Look for richness of coloring, size, shape, substance, and arrangement of flowers on the inflorescence. In miniatures, the bottom flower should clear the leaf mass and have two or three sprays of flowers.

The AOS Awards

Let us look at some of the AOS awards so we have a better understanding of what they are. The first is known as the HCC/AOS or Highly Commended Certificate. A minimum of 75 points is required for this award. The point spread for an HCC is from 75 to 79.5. The next award in ascending order is the Award of Merit, AM/AOS. The plant must score from 80 to 89.5. This is a coveted award which is given only to plants of exceptional beauty and outstanding qualities. The next and highest award the American Orchid Society can give to an orchid, is the First Class Certificate of FCC/AOS. A score of 90 points or more is required. Very few orchids ever receive an FCC/AOS. In order to receive 90 points or higher, the orchid must be superior in so many qualities, such as brilliance of coloring, larger size flowers, and exceptionally fine shape with flowers well carried on a good strong stem.

There are other awards of which the amateur should know. One which is especially important to those who favor the species is the award known as the Certificate of Horticultural Merit. It is granted to a species orchid which is notable for its charm and beauty and which could be used for hybridizing or which has desirable qualities beyond being unusual, odd, or rare. The Certificate of Cultural Merit is an award given to plants shown by an exhibitor which have been grown to special size and beauty and show excellence of culture. Basically the award is transient in that, while a particular plant which has received this award will carry the CCM on all divisions, the award is granted to that plant at the moment of its specimen culture. The division carry-

Phalaenopsis Misty Moon is the recipient of several AOS awards.

ing the symbols of a cultural award does tell you that particular variety lends itself to specimen culture.

Of special value to those interested in finer orchids and in understanding the award system is the American Orchid Society's Awards Quarterly. This publication lists all AOS awards with illustrations. It is not only very educational and interesting but it is a wonderful "want list" to those who desire to build a collection of superior orchids of award quality.

While a system of awards is invaluable and indispensable, it must be used in conjunction with your basic appreciation of beauty. Most people who raise orchids appreciate beautiful flowers and do not need to run a plant through a series of measurements and tests to determine whether or not it is beautiful. Within us all, we have the basic ability to look at something and, within our own minds, determine whether or not we consider it beautiful. If we let ourselves be governed

too much by rigidity of thinking and by what we are supposed to like, it can destroy our basic appreciation of beauty.

It has been my observation that the general public, those who come into an orchid nursery and look at the flowers, are often just as capable of spotting a fine orchid or one of award potential as the best trained judge. The average person will look at a flower and give what we could call a "gut response." Very often this is quite accurate. When something like this is then submitted for judging, it goes through a more scientific and expert appraisal. This confirms for the record books the superior qualities of the plant and that the plant is worthy of an award.

While an award system definitely has its place, the majority of orchids, while not of award caliber, are beautiful.

It is also important to know that many awarded orchids are fine parents, however, many famous orchid parents have never received awards. 🌷

Orchid societies and their shows provide an opportunity for you to share information and have your plants judged.

WHY JOIN AN ORCHID SOCIETY?

JANET HOWE

In the United States, if you walk into an average florist shop or nursery and ask for orchid plants, you'll possibly be shown a tiny selection of cattleyas, cymbidiums, phalaenopsis, and/or paphiopedilums at inflated prices, and receive indifferent or incorrect instructions for culture.

If you hope to grow more than two or three orchid plants on your windowsills, under lights, or in your greenhouse, membership in a local, regional, national, or international orchid society is your "Open Sesame" to the wonderful world of what has been estimated to be approximately 17,000 species of these intriguing plants (some still undiscovered). In addition to the species, there are many, many thousands of man-made hybrids with registered parentage and complex bloodlines dating back to 1852 when the first orchid hybrid was made in England.

I joined my first orchid society, the Greater New York Orchid Society, because I'd heard that members' own surplus plants were sold at reasonable prices, before every 8 p.m. program. Every fourth Wednesday of the month at the Snuff Mill of the New York Botanical Garden in the Bronx, members gathered at 7 p.m. to sell and trade plants and supplies. Back then, dues per year for either an individual or family membership were barely enough to pay for the monthly newsletter plus the coffee and Danish served at meetings. This is still the case for many local orchid societies. For the small annual fee, one also is afforded the opportunity to meet fellow orchid lovers, both amateur and professional.

The Greater New York Orchid Society

JANET HOWE *reviews orchid books and writes orchid "chats" for several orchid society magazines.*

monthly meetings, like other local societies in any metropolitan area, offer cultural information by advanced growers, slide programs given by qualified speakers on many aspects of orchid growing, collecting, conserving, hybridizing, or whatever you always wanted to know about orchids but didn't know whom to ask. Informal roundtable discussions on every facet of the hobby are another feature of monthly local society meetings.

Many societies hold an annual auction at which superb orchids (both donated and purchased) are offered to the highest bidders. They have a show table at every meeting and awards are given deserving plants . . . great for the ego if your plant is selected, a learning session even if it's not. Experienced growers extend their hands whenever novices encounter problems.

The American Orchid Society, with more than 400 local or regional affiliated societies, is headquartered at 6000 South Olive Ave., West Palm Beach, Florida 33405. The AOS is international in scope. Meetings are held twice a year in designated American cities.

Meetings, however, are not the main reason for joining the American Orchid Society. Its monthly publication, the *American Orchid Society Bulletin*, is. For $20 a year, members of AOS receive twelve issues of one of the biggest magazine bargains extant. It features color-illustrated articles by knowledgeable writers on every topic dear to an orchidophile's heart, notes on new orchid books, announcements of coming shows and special events, and regular departments such as Speaking Orchid-wise, the Question Box, and New Orchid Hybrids (reprinted from the English *Orchid Review*).

Interesting as these sections are, true hobbyists turn first to the ads and read the Bulletin from back to front, eager to learn what's new where.

Why join an orchid society? The answer is almost impossible to put into words because it's never exactly the same experience for any two individuals. Personally, although I was intimidated by all the talk of this mericlone and that back-bulb for almost a year after I joined my first society, I'm now able to give lectures to horticultural societies and garden clubs, and as the detergent ad says, "That's an improvement."

Members of the American Orchid Society receive the color-illustrated *Orchids*, a monthly magazine containing articles ranging from basic cultural techniques to scientific surveys of orchid genera. Members of the AOS also receive an AOS almanac, as well as a complementary copy of *Your First Orchid*. In 1997, the annual dues in the U.S. were $36 for a single membership and $46 for a joint membership. Non-U.S. single memberships were $42.

The AOS works with more than 500 affiliated societies located throughout the U.S.A. and many other countries. Various AOS committees function internationally in the fields of education and research, conservation, orchid history, and awards. The AOS is a sponsor of the triennial World Orchid Conferences. Monthly AOS judgings take place at various judging centers throughout the continental U.S. and Hawaii. Schedules for the official judgings are listed in AOS publications. For information on current membership rates and benefits contact:

AMERICAN ORCHID SOCIETY
6000 SOUTH OLIVE AVENUE
WEST PALM BEACH, FL 33405-4199
PHONE (561) 585-8666
FAX (561) 585-0654

WORLD ORCHID CONFERENCES

Stanhopea wardii

Every three years the international orchid community stages a World Orchid Conference. Each conference is held in a different country but always in a nation where the active local orchid societies are filled with energetic members receptive to visitors from abroad. An elaborate orchid show is the highlight of every World Orchid Conference.

Visit a World Orchid Conference for an exciting introduction to orchid growing. Orchid experts from many countries present programs related to current research and all aspects of orchid growing. Commercial displays offer the latest hybrids and rare species grown from seed and by tissue culture. Various products useful in orchid culture are on sale.

Most conferences include a special show section devoted to art. Here orchid paintings, sculpture, ceramics, and similar representations of orchids by professional and amateur artists are exhibited, judged, and awarded. In the main show section orchid flowers, plants, and whole displays of live blooming orchids are evaluated by judging teams who award an array of cups, ribbons, plates, and plaques.

Visitors gather at the seventh World Orchid Conference
in Medellin, Colombia.

Local society members offer home visits with hobby growers, the official conference travel agents arrange side-trips to places of interest, and commercial firms welcome conference registrants with special tours through their establishments.

In the past, World Orchid Conferences have been in widely differing locations around the globe, including Tokyo, Japan, Rio de Janeiro, Brazil, New Zealand, Bangkok, Thailand, and Miami, Florida. These conferences offer you an excellent opportunity to learn more about orchids on an international level. The American Orchid Society (see page 82) is the best source of information about future conferences. 🍃

[C.M.F.]

SOURCES OF ORCHID PLANTS AND GROWING SUPPLIES

everal large commercial orchid ranges in the United States offer good assortments of popular genera and the supplies required to grow them. Other smaller orchid nurseries, although offering mail-order service, specialize in a limited number of genera or specific types of orchids such as cool growers or miniatures. Local garden supply stores offer some supplies used in growing orchids but the proper potting media for orchids are difficult to find in some regions. You may order potting media and mixtures from the large commercial nurseries listed here. Some local orchid societies accommodate members by pooling orders for growing supplies, thus saving postage. Botanical garden shops often carry small quantities of potting mix for orchids.

Listed here are a few of the larger orchid firms. For an extensive display of current orchid firm ads please consult a copy of the American Orchid Society *AOS Bulletin*. Firms listed below are experienced in mail-order shipping of orchids but requesting shipment to areas below freezing during the winter increases the risk that orchids will be damaged. For the most secure shipment to states with cold winters request delivery between April and November.

Carter and Holmes Orchids
629 Mendenhall Rd., P.O. Box 668
Newberry, SC 29108
(803) 276-0579

Orchids by Hausermann, Inc.
2N134 Addison Rd.
Villa Park, IL 60181
(630) 543-6855

Rod McLellan Co.
1450 El Camino Real
South San Francisco, CA 94080
(415) 871-5655

Stewart Orchids
3376 Foothill Rd.
Carpinteria, CA 93013
(805) 684-5448

Zuma Canyon Orchids
5949 Bonsall Drive
Malibu, CA 90265
(310) 457-9771

OVERSEAS SOURCES
IN THE TROPICS

Many overseas orchid sources are located in tropical countries where orchids are native. The modern trend is for commercial firms to select the best clones of indigenous species, then grow more from seed and/or meristem culture. International regulations require that all orchids entering the United States be accompanied by official CITES documents, conforming to the USA's agreement to cooperate with laws to protect endangered species. Orchids sent to the U.S. without the required documentation (Certificate of Origin and CITES papers from the country of origin) will be confiscated by the U.S. Agricultural Inspectors at port of entry. The overseas orchid growers listed below are some of the established firms that are prepared to send all CITES required documentation with their export plant shipments. Note that to import orchids from overseas you will also need a permit from the U.S. Department of Agriculture, available free from the USDA (Permit Unit, USDA, APHIS, PPQ, Federal Bldg., Rm. 368, Hyattsville MD 20782).

Green Orchids (Mr. Shat Lun Cheng)
P.O. Box 7-587, Taipei, Taiwan
Meristems of outstanding cattleyas and phalaenopsis. $5.00 color catalog.

Kabukiran Orchids (Mr. & Mrs. Javier)
P.O. Box 744
Quezon City, Philippines
Philippine species, $1.00 catalog.

Kanjana Orchids
372/1 Soi 28 Phaholyothin Road
Bangkhean, Bangkok 10900 Thailand
Free Catalog offers modern tropical hybrids in several genera.

Ooi Leng Sun Orchids
(Mr. Michael Ooi)
873 Sungei Dua
Butterworth, Wellesley, Malayasia
Malayasian species and their hybrids.
Free catalog.

T. Orchids
(Mr. Thonglor)
P.O. Box 21-19
Bangkok 21, Thailand
Hybrid dendrobiums and vandaceous types plus Thai species. $5.00 color catalog.

FURTHER READING

Culture

All About Orchids by Charles Marden Fitch. Doubleday and Co., New York. Complete guide to modern cultural techniques, hybrids, international sources of plants.

Handbook on Orchid Culture by the American Orchid Society. A booklet covering basics of orchid culture. Available from AOS.

Miniature Orchids by Rebecca Northern. Van Nostrand Reinhold Co., New York. Small-growing orchids for the home.

Orchid Culture Under Lights by Richard Peterson. Indoor Light Gardening Society of America. An illustrated 19-page paper-back booklet available from the Indoor Gardening Society, 128 W. 58th St., New York, NY 10019.

The Paphiopedilum Grower's Manual by Lance A. Birk. A book written for the orchid fancier who wants to learn everything there is to know about the Lady Slipper orchids. Available from the author at 1721 Las Canoas Rd., Santa Barbara, CA 93105.

Reference

Encyclopaedia of Cultivated Orchids by Alex D. Hawkes. Faber and Faber Ltd., London. Includes some culture notes.

Orchid Biology, Reviews and Perspectives edited by Joseph Arditti. Cornell University Press, Ithaca, NY. Advanced scientific papers.

The Manual of Cultivated Orchid Species by Bechtel, Cribb, and Launet. MIT Press, Cambridge, MA. Many color photos.

The Orchids, Scientific Studies edited by Carl L. Withner. John Wiley & Sons, New York. Research papers collected, illustrated.

Handbook on Orchid Pests and Diseases. Useful paperback from The American Orchid Society. Most recent edition is available directly from the AOS office. Revised in 1985.

GLOSSARY OF ORCHID TERMS

The glossary presented here is in no sense comprehensive. It contains essentially those terms which the reader of the foregoing articles might find difficult or confusing. Botanical terms should not be frightening; they are exact and once a grower becomes accustomed to them, they are invaluable in discussions of one's orchids.

Award initials. The FCC/AOS, AM/AOS, etc., which may follow an orchid's name. See "Benefits of the AOS Awards System" (page 82) for explanation.

Back bulb. One of the older *pseudobulbs* on an orchid plant, suitable for use in propagation.

"Botanical." Orchid-growers' slang for all small or non-showy kinds of orchids, in contrast to the commercial corsage types of orchids. For the most part, these are grown and hybridized by hobbyists. (A better term is needed.)

Callus. An area at the base of the lip of the orchid flower that apparently is attractive to insects. Among orchid specialists it provides a diagnostic character for differentiating species.

Clone. All the plants derived by successive vegetative propagation, beginning with one original plant. In writing, the clonal name is set off in single quotation marks.

Column. The unique reproductive structure found only in the orchid family. The *stamens* are generally reduced to one or two (occasionally three are present) and are fused with the *style* and *stigma* of the *pistil*.

Community pot. Often referred to as a "compot." The single pot or other container in which orchid seedlings are planted in groups of 15 to 20 after removal from the sterile culture bottle in which they were first sown.

Corm. A solid, bulblike, fleshy base of a stem, common to many terrestrial orchid species.

Crocks. Another word for pot-sherds—pieces of broken flower pots which are placed in the bottom of a pot for drainage.

Cultivar. A race of plants, originated and maintained in cultivation for unusual or desirable qualities and given a special name. Distinct from a species.

Deciduous. Literally, *falling off*; used of plants which drop their leaves seasonally.

Epiphyte. Literally, *on a plant*; one plant which grows upon another, but *not as a parasite*. An epiphyte merely perches on the trunk or branches of its dwelling place—usually a tree.

Grex. All the sibling plants produced by hybridizing two species, a species and a hybrid, or two different hybrids.

Hapuu. Hawaiian tree fern (*Cibotium glaucum* or *C. chamissoi*). The aerial roots, which surround the trunk in a thick, matted layer, are used as a potting medium for orchids.

Keiki. Hawaiian word meaning a child or little one, used as a name for the off-shoots or plantlets that develop from the main stem or on old flower spikes of certain orchid species. After their roots have developed they may be separated from the mother plant and grown as new individuals.

Labellum. The lip of an orchid flower, formed by one of the three petals.

Lead. A new growth arising on a sympodial orchid.

Mericlone. A plant produced by "meristeming."

Meristem. As a noun, *meristem* refers to embryonic tissue, the cells of which are capable of active division. As a verb, it is orchid-growers' slang for the method of propagation by which the apical cells are removed from an orchid shoot tip and grown on, by continued division, as individual plants. A plant produced by this method is called a *mericlone*.

Monopodial. One of the two types of growth habits in plants. (Compare *sympodial*.) *Mono*, meaning *one*, gives a clue to the meaning of the word. Monopodial orchids have only one stem, which grows continuously from the apex, on and on. As the stem elongates and produces leaves and flowers, roots come not only from the base, but usually also from the stem itself.

Osmunda. Roots of ferns of the genus *Osmunda*, used as a potting medium.

Ovary. The part of the *pistil* that bears the bodies (ovules) which can become seeds when fertilized. In an orchid flower the ovary is situated *beneath* the sepals and petals.

Pistil. The female reproductive structure of flower, consisting of *stigma, style* and *ovary*. In an orchid flower, stigma, and style are fused with the *stamens* into a *column*.

Pollen. The male reproductive cells in a flower; in an orchid flower, usually borne on the *column* in a coherent mass called a *pollinium* (plural: *pollinia*).

Protocorm. The stage of growth of an orchid seedling before any leaves or roots have become differentiated. The minute embryo in the seed will have developed only into a little ball of cells.

Pseudobulb. A solid, bulbous enlargement of the lower part of the secondary stems, common among *epiphytic* orchids.

Rhizome. In general botanical parlance, a horizontal primary stem, either underground or at the soil surface. In *epiphytic orchids*, which grow on tree branches and other non-granular surfaces, there is no surrounding soil. In *sympodial* orchids, the rhizome connects successive growths, the distance between which varies in different species from a fraction of an inch to two feet.

Selfing. Pollinating a flower with its own pollen. While self-pollinating is usually avoided in the orchid family, it is sometimes desirable to increase the number of plants in a given strain or to maintain a certain group of genetic traits.

Semi-alba. A descriptive word of commercial coinage used to designate a cattleya hybrid with white sepals, two white petals and a colored lip.

Stamen. Male reproductive organ in a flower, bearing at its tip the fertilizing cells called *pollen*. In an orchid flower, incorporated into the *column*.

Stigmatic surface. That part of the *column* of an orchid flower which receives the pollen. It corresponds to the *stigma* of flowers in other families.

Style. The stalk of the *pistil* which connects the *stigma*, at the tip, with the *ovary*, at the base. In an orchid flower, the *style* is incorporated into the *column*.

Sympodial. One of the two types of growth habits in plants. (Compare *monopodial*.) In sympodial growth, the apex of a stem does not continue growth; instead, growth is resumed by a bud below the apex (in an orchid, generally on the rhizome) which repeats the process. As a sympodial orchid puts out new growth periodically at its base, it "walks" along year after year, growth after growth.

Tepals. Sepals and petals of a flower when they are similar in form and color.

Terete leaves. Fleshy, cylindrical leaves which taper to a point. They can vary from the size of slender knitting needles to that of big cigars.

Velamen. The white, thick, spongy, absorbing and anchoring layer of cells that covers all but the growing tip of the aerial roots of orchids.

Xerophytic. Adapted to a dry environment, with succulent, wax-covered leaves and fleshy stems being the usual modifications. Most epiphytic orchids show one or more such adaptations, as do cacti and other succulent plants.

INDEX

94

Gardening Books
FOR THE
Next Century

Published four times a year,
these award-winning books explore the
frontiers of ecological gardening.
Your subscription to BBG's **21st-Century
Gardening Series** is free with
Brooklyn Botanic Garden membership.

TO BECOME A MEMBER

please call (718) 622-4433, ext. 265.
Or, photocopy this form,
complete and return to:
Membership Department, Brooklyn Botanic Garden,
1000 Washington Avenue, Brooklyn, NY 11225-1099

YOUR NAME . . . .

ADDRESS . . . .

CITY/STATE/ZIP . . . .

PHONE . . . .

I want to subscribe to the 21st-Century Gardening Series
(4 quarterly volumes) by becoming a member of the
Brooklyn Botanic Garden:

☐ **$35 · SUBSCRIBER**   ☐ **$125 · SIGNATURE**

☐ **$50 · FAMILY/DUAL**   ☐ **$300 · SPONSOR**

TOTAL $ . . . .

FORM OF PAYMENT:

☐ CHECK ENCLOSED   ☐ VISA   ☐ MASTERCARD

CREDIT CARD# . . . .

EXP . . . .

SIGNATURE . . . .